THE BLACK HOLOCAUST

FOR BEGINNERS

by S.E. Anderson

80 MILLION

illustrated by The Cro-maat Collective & Vanessa Holley

Writers and Readers

WRITERS AND READERS PUBLISHING, INC.

P.O. Box 461, Village Station
New York, NY 10014

Writers and Readers Limited
9 Cynthia Street
London N1 9JF
England
•

Text Copyright: © 1995, S.E. Anderson
Illustrations © 1995, The Cro-maat Collective; Vanessa Holley
Cover Art © 1995, Vanessa Holley
Cover & Book Design: Terrie Dunkelberger
Elmina Castle photos by Chris Burns

A Writers and Readers Documentary Comic Book
Copyright © 1995
ISBN # 0-86316-178-2
1 2 3 4 5 6 7 8 9 0

Manufactured in the United States of America

Beginners Documentary Comic Books are published by
Writers and Readers Publishing, Inc. Its trademark, consisting of the words "For Beginners, Writers and Readers
Documentary Comic Books" and the Writers and Readers
logo, is registered in the U. S. Patent and Trademark Office
and in other countries.

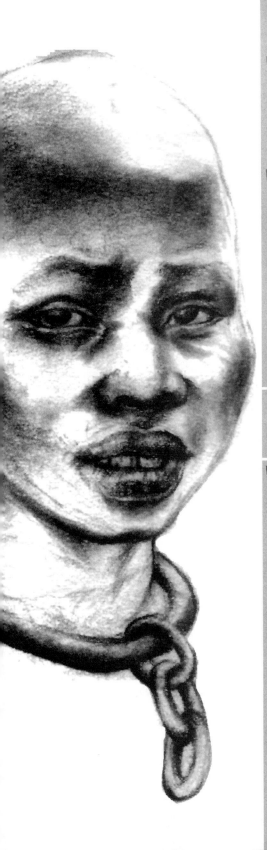

To the tens of millions of African captives who gave their lives but not their Spirits to the MiddlePassage—

To Quashey, Harriet, Cinque, Sojourner, Fannie Lou, Nat, Malcolm, RubyDoris, Gabriel, Walter, Dessaline, Tituba, Marcus, Cuffey... all our Heroes and Sheroes who gave their lives but not their Spirits to the FreedomStruggle—

To Dedan, Marc, Alicia, Kikuya, Asha, Fanon, Carlos... the last of the 20th Century FreedomFighters—

To Nandi, Ola Bijan, Camilo, Amilcar... the first of the 21st Century FreedomFighters—

To our Parents for their wisdom and guidance to now—

To our Soulmates Comrades Lovers for their strength, direction and perseverance—

To Assata: The Soul of the Black Liberation Movement—

(side list: among the more expendable)

as another way of drawing more attention
to those of us who seldom sit
much less ever get to do that here
i offer you this sidelist
elements of which are almost as old
as ass whippin itself.

footsoldier infantry veteran guard
haystacker gladiator blacksmith serf
peon sharecropper tenant farmer robbed
bricklayer carpenter protege boot
ryot eunuch esne servant maid
stoker valet gardener page
chamberwork butler chimney sweep cook
busted & harnessed or pressed in through jail
architect villain untoughables teach
railsplitter chain gang operate compute
attendant painter typist on hand
doormat subject homeless abject bum
beaten broken rowing & raped
ayah automaton watchdog killed
jibaro guajiro cimarron maroon
outlyer runaway geisha gullah jack
fieldhand driver footman caught
coolie miner trampled whore
vassal helot citizen churl
felahin cleaning lady washerwoman slave.

—poem by Louis Reyes Rivera
From *Scattered Scripture*

TABLE OF CONTENTS

SANKOFA: WE LOOK TO THE PAST TO HELP US MOVE FORWARD INTO THE FUTURE.

Remembrance has not escaped us
— Ayi Kwei Armah

vi

HOLOCAUST

FOR BEGINNERS

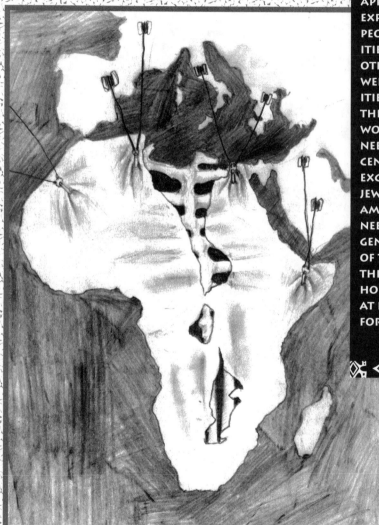

THE GREEK WORD "HOLOCAUST"...SHOULD REMAIN A GENERIC METAPHOR AND BE APPLICABLE TO THE EXPERIENCE OF OTHER PEOPLE, UNDER ATROCITIES PERPETRATED BY OTHER SYSTEMS, AS WELL AS TO THE ATROCITIES OF THE NAZIS. THE GREEK-DERIVED WORD "HOLOCAUST" NEED NOT BE JUDEO-CENTRIC—RESERVED EXCLUSIVELY FOR THE JEWISH EXPERIENCE. AMERICAN CHILDREN NEED TO KNOW THAT GENOCIDE WAS PART OF THE BIRTH OF THIS NATION. THE HOLOCAUST BEGAN AT HOME— "LEST WE FORGET!"

—ALI MAZURI

THE BLACK HOLOCAUST
FOR BEGINNERS

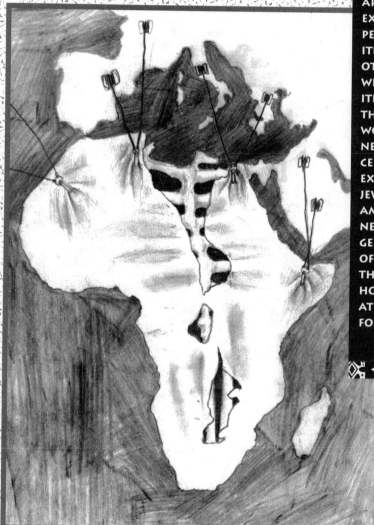

THE GREEK WORD "HOLOCAUST"...SHOULD REMAIN A GENERIC METAPHOR AND BE APPLICABLE TO THE EXPERIENCE OF OTHER PEOPLE, UNDER ATROCITIES PERPETRATED BY OTHER SYSTEMS, AS WELL AS TO THE ATROCITIES OF THE NAZIS. THE GREEK-DERIVED WORD "HOLOCAUST" NEED NOT BE JUDEO-CENTRIC—RESERVED EXCLUSIVELY FOR THE JEWISH EXPERIENCE. AMERICAN CHILDREN NEED TO KNOW THAT GENOCIDE WAS PART OF THE BIRTH OF THIS NATION. THE HOLOCAUST BEGAN AT HOME— "LEST WE FORGET!"

—ALI MAZURI

INTRODUCTION

THE MEANING AND IMPORTANCE OF THE BLACK HOLOCAUST

This book is about an unimaginable experience that actually happened to tens of millions of Africans. This book is a **starting point** for anyone who wants to know about the development of racism, capitalism, and the resulting pillage and plunder of Africa. This book is about **never forgetting** that experience. This book is a beginner's guide to how Africans in the Americas came to be. It's about locating the stolen cultural and political heritage buried in the complex and beastly acts of the Slave Trade.

African Americans are a captured people rather than a conquered people — since they were forcibly exported from their homes in Africa. The captivity and enslavement of free African people began long before the August 1619 arrival in the port of Jamestown, Virginia of "Angela"—the first African woman to set foot on North American shores—after being held Captive on board the *Treasurer*; or with (on that same day) the docking of the creaky and seaworn Dutch ship the *Cathy Constant*, carrying the surviving "20-odd Africans" out of the original 100 captives as North America's first enslaved Africans.

The enslavement of free Africans began long before 1619, and, as we shall see, it was not confined to North America— it was *global*.

Above all, this book is about an unreported *genocide*—the one thousand two hundred year *Black Holocaust*.

THE TOTAL NUMBER OF SLAVES IMPORTED IS NOT KNOWN. IT IS ESTIMATED THAT NEARLY 900,000 CAME TO AMERICA IN THE SIXTEENTH CENTURY, 2.75 MILLION IN THE SEVENTEENTH CENTURY, 7 MILLION IN THE EIGHTEENTH, AND OVER 4 MILLION IN THE NINETEENTH — PERHAPS 15 MILLION IN TOTAL.

PROBABLY EVERY SLAVE IMPORTED REPRESENTED, ON THE AVERAGE, FIVE CORPSES IN AFRICA OR ON THE HIGH SEAS. THE AMERICAN SLAVE TRADE, THEREFORE, MEANT THE ELIMINATION OF AT LEAST 60 MILLION AFRICANS.
— ARMET FRANCIS: *The Black Triangle*

PART 1:

THE REAL HISTORICAL FOUNDATIONS OF AFRICAN CIVILIZATION & SLAVERY

LET US BEGIN WITH A FEW *REAL* ANSWERS TO OLD QUESTIONS

The Slave trade was not a statistic, however astronomical. The slave trade was people living, lying, stealing, murdering, dying. The slave trade was a black man who stepped out of his house for a breath of fresh air and ended up, ten months later, in Georgia with bruises on his back and a brand on his chest.

The slave trade was a black mother suffocating her new-born baby because she didn't want him to grow up to be a slave.

The slave trade was a "kind" captain forcing his suicide-minded passengers to eat by breaking their teeth, though, as he said, he was "naturally compassionate."

The slave trade was a bishop sitting on an ivory chair on a wharf in the Congo and extending his fat hand in wholesale baptism of slaves who were rowed beneath him, going in chains to the slave ships.

The slave trade was a greedy [African] king raiding his own villages to get slaves to buy brandy.

The slave trade was a pious captain holding prayer services twice a day on his slave ship and writing later the famous hymn: "How Sweet the Name of Jesus Sounds."

The slave trade was deserted villages, bleached bones on slave trails and people with no last names. It was Caesar negro, Anglo negro and Negro Mary....

—**Lerone Bennett:** *Before the Mayflower*

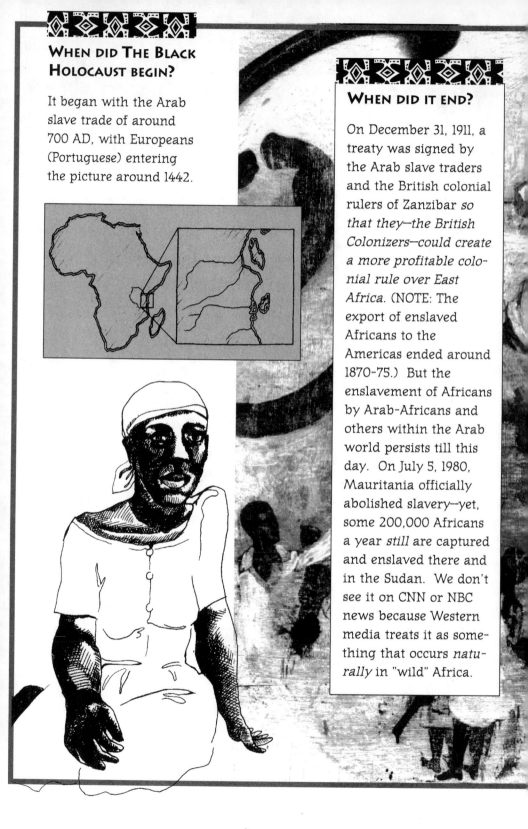

WHEN DID THE BLACK HOLOCAUST BEGIN?

It began with the Arab slave trade of around 700 AD, with Europeans (Portuguese) entering the picture around 1442.

WHEN DID IT END?

On December 31, 1911, a treaty was signed by the Arab slave traders and the British colonial rulers of Zanzibar *so that they—the British Colonizers—could create a more profitable colonial rule over East Africa.* (NOTE: The export of enslaved Africans to the Americas ended around 1870-75.) But the enslavement of Africans by Arab-Africans and others within the Arab world persists till this day. On July 5, 1980, Mauritania officially abolished slavery—yet, some 200,000 Africans a year *still* are captured and enslaved there and in the Sudan. We don't see it on CNN or NBC news because Western media treats it as something that occurs *naturally* in "wild" Africa.

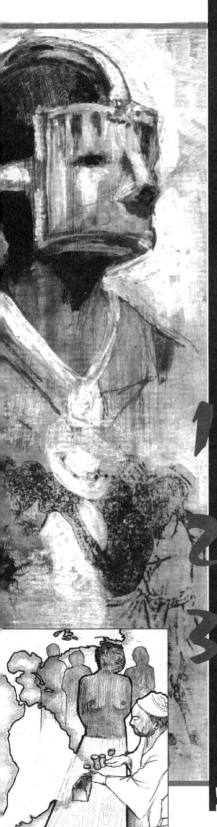

"THE AFRICAN SLAVE TRADE: 1995"

African Americans...are comforted only by the assurance that the buying and selling of Black Africans ended in the distant past. But such a belief is myth.

It has become clear that the enslavement of Black Africans did not stop with the demise of the Atlantic Slave Trade. That on this very day and hour, as you read this, there are Black people being bought and sold in two North African countries [Mauritania & Sudan].

"Routine punishments for the slightest fault include beatings, denial of food and prolonged exposure to the sun, with hands and feet tied together. Serious infringement of the master's rule can mean prolonged tortures, as documented in a report by *Africa Watch*. These include:

The **'camel treatment,'** where a human being is wrapped around the belly of a dehydrated camel and tied there. The camel is then given water to drink until its belly expands enough to tear the slave apart.

The **'insect treatment,'** where insects are put into a person's ears. The ears are waxed shut. The arms and legs are bound. The person goes insane from the bugs running around in his head.

The **'burning coals,'** where the victim is sealed flat, with his legs spread out. He is then buried in sand up to his waist until he cannot move. Coals are placed between his legs and are burnt slowly. After a while, the legs, thighs, and sex of the victim are burnt. There are other gruesome tortures— none of which is fit to describe in a family newspaper" states *Africa Watch*."
—**Samuel Cotton,** *The City SUN* [Feb.7,1995]

How many Africans were enslaved?
20 – 40 million.

Did they go passively or did they resist?
Despite the great odds against them, they fought their captors at every turn.
That is why so many of them died.

How many Africans died during the 1400 years of the Holocaust?
50 – 80 million.

What part of the Africa continent was affected by the Black Holocaust?
All of Africa.

Were Africans always enslaved by whites and Arabs?
    NO!

Were and are people of African descent less intelligent than white folks?
    Of course not!

Did white Europeans "discover" Africans swinging from trees in the "jungles" of Africa and bring them "civilization?"
    Of course not! (Unless virtual genocide is your idea of "civilization.")

Were Africans steeped in superstition and ignorant of Science & Technology?
    Of course not!

Humanity had its beginnings in Africa more than 3 million years ago with the first beings to walk upright and have opposable thumbs to grab and control sticks and stones as extensions of the hand. In other words, Africans invented tools and weapons to help themselves not only survive but thrive as well. To this date, the earliest bones of human beings were and are still being found in the Olduvai Gorge in east Africa, a region covering an area almost as big as the United States.

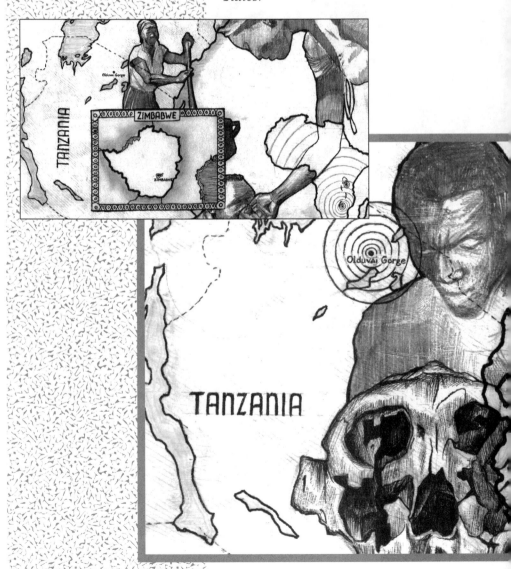

Over a million years ago, humans began migrating out of the Olduvai Gorge region in search of food and shelter. Others stayed in the rich, fertile regions around the Nile Valley, which runs through Africa for thousands of miles (longer than the distance between New York and Los Angeles!). About 250,000 years ago, early Africans began a major diet shift that helped increase brain size. They began to live longer (to about 40 years), walk more upright, create larger and more complex social relations which, in turn, helped them have more babies that survived to adulthood.

Around 50,000 years ago, some of these extended families and clans began to settle around the southern region of the Olduvai Gorge and began to establish control over their food—*farming!* They discovered the relationships between soil, rain, rivers, sun and phases of the moon and living things. This settling down gave them more time to think about their world and the universe around them. Men and women were engaged in this effort to understand everything. Eventually, men became the dominant figures within their societies (although there were exceptions found in Africa and elsewhere where women were the dominant political force). Social relations become even more complex, and a hierarchy developed, i.e., priests and priestesses who possessed knowledge of Nature and divine rulers; "average" men and women who had to work long, hard hours to compensate for those who did not work.

We have evidence of one of these early, highly developed societies in a region we call Zimbabwe today. It is a **FACT that Africans were smelting iron some 40,000 years ago!** (That is <u>not</u> a misprint! Smelting was done in the area now called Tanzania, not far south of the Olduvai Gorge, the location of L.S.B. Leakey's findings of the earliest humanoid skulls.) Smelting iron requires a serious division of labor (miners, farmers, metalworkers, hunters...), an apprenticeship educational system, excellent hunting techniques and weaponry, and knowledge of how and where to trade.

This knowledge and culture spread north along the rivers and valleys that flowed into the Nile River. After about 20,000 more years of learning through trial and error and observation, the Africans of the Nubian/Kush region (today we call it the Sudan, Ethiopia, Eritrea, Somalia) developed a very sophisticated civilization. This is not to say that there were no other equally sophisticated civilizations. Rather, to date, we have more archaeological evidence of the Kush people than, say, the Ishongo people of the Congo region or the people of Zimbabwe. What we do know about this region of Africa is that for thousands of years the people developed their intellect and knowledge of Nature to such a high degree that by 5000B.C., the Nubians, Kushites, and Egyptians knew of the Earth's spherical shape, its approximate size, along with basic knowledge of gravity and the existence of north/south magnetic poles.

They were engineers unrivaled even today! They were master chemists, biologists, physicians, mathematicians, spiritualists. And they were Black. BLACK. Look at the evidence!

At the same time, other African civilizations were struggling, growing, and fighting for land and labor during the time of the Pharaohs.

(We are just beginning to learn about them because African historians and archaeologists now have the chance to research and study these early civilizations.)

They traded and fought with Egypt and peoples of Asia, from Bagdad to Bombay to Beijing. Africans—particularly from the region we now call Kenya and Tanzania—even traded with the "Aborigines" of Australia and the peoples of the South Pacific, beginning in the 1100s (A.D.) and continuing for thousands of years.

(In fact, all you have to do is look at the people and their cultural works and see the heavy influence of Africa!)

East Africans of the "Swahili" culture (a blend of the Arab and indigenous African cultures that emerged around 900A.D.), during the late 1300s and 1400s, traded extensively with the Chinese— particularly with Emperor Zhu Di, who had created a great fleet, with ships four and five times the size of European ships of the same period! It would take the West another six hundred years to develop the technological know-how to build ships with watertight bulkhead compartments!

> "...AT THE PORT OF QUANZHOU ON THE FUJIAN COAST, [ITALIAN ADVENTURER/MERCHANT] MARCO POLO, WHO STAYED AT THE KHAN'S COURT FROM 1275 TO 1292, SAW FOUR-MATSTED OCEANGOING JUNKS WITH NO FEWER THAN 60 INDIVIDUAL CABINS FOR MERCHANTS.... . THE SHIPS CARRIED 150 TO 300 CREWMEN, AND THEY HAD WATERTIGHT BULKHEAD COMPARTMENTS...."
>
> —LOUISE LEVATHES: *When China Ruled the Seas* - 1994

By the 1400s the Chinese had developed their shipbuilding technology to such an extent that many of their oceangoing vessels were more than 400 feet long and 200 feet wide! Moreover, the oceangoing trading fleet to East Africa (commanded by the eunuch admiral Zheng He) in 1418, for example, was made up of a huge entourage of ...

> "...LARGE JUNKS [AND] NEARLY A HUNDRED SUPPLY SHIPS, [FRESH] WATER TANKERS, TRANSPORTS FOR CALVARY HORSES, WARSHIPS AND MULTIOARED BOATS NUMBERING UP TO 28,000 SAILORS AND SOLDIERS. IT WAS A UNIQUE ARMADA IN THE HISTORY OF CHINA— AND THE WORLD— NOT TO BE SURPASSED UNTIL THE INVASION FLEETS OF WORLD WAR I SAILED THE SEAS.
>
> IN 1498, WHEN VASCO DA GAMA AND HIS FLEET OF THREE BATTERED CARAVELS ROUNDED THE CAPE OF GOOD HOPE AND LANDED IN EAST AFRICA.... THE AFRICANS SCOFFED AT THE TRINKETS THE PORTUGUESE OFFERED...AND SEEMED UNIMPRESSED WITH THEIR SMALL SHIPS."
>
> —LEVATHES: *When China Ruled the Seas*

By July 15, 1419 Admiral Zheng He returned to China with numerous African Ambassadors who began to negotiate trade relations with China and their respective kingdoms. But it was also known by these African ambassadors that the Chinese Emperors not only kept Chinese slaves, but also thousands of African slaves.

"The Tang emperors [618A.D. to 960A.D.] were...great admirers of Korean women...for imperial harems. Dwarfs and pygmies...were prized human cargo, as were black slaves from...the east coast of Africa....

THE EXTENT OF THE CHINA SLAVE TRADE IS DIFFICULT TO DETERMINE.... AFRICAN SLAVES WERE TREATED LITTLE BETTER THAN BEASTS OF BURDEN. THEY WERE MADE TO LIFT HEAVY WEIGHTS AND, BECAUSE THE CHINESE BELEIVED THEY SWAM 'WITHOUT BLINKING THEIR EYES,' WERE EMPLOYED AS DIVERS TO REPAIR LEAKING BOATS. MANY MUST HAVE...DIED SOON AFTER ARRIVAL IN CHINA.... . BUT, 'IF THEY DO NOT DIE, ONE CAN KEEP THEM, AND AFTER HAVING BEEN KEPT A LONG TIME THEY BEGIN TO UNDERSTAND THE LANGUAGE OF HUMAN BEINGS, THOUGH THEMSELVES CANNOT SPEAK IT.'"

—LEVATHES: *When China Ruled the Seas*

For centuries the Chinese ruling classes had racist and chauvinistic views toward *all* nonChinese people. Unlike European capitalists, they did not *systematically* and *consciously* seek out a people to label subhuman for the purpose of increasing their profits.

In addition to the Chinese connection, there is evidence that the people of Africa even traded with the indigenous folk of the Americas, hundreds of years before the Europeans invaded them.

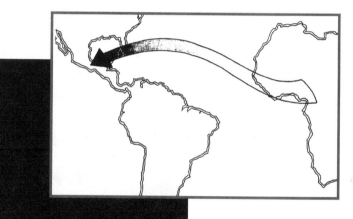

REMEMBER...

Africa TRADED with the Americas— It didn't INVADE Them!

When the newly formed European nations finally began to get their political and economic act together in the 1400s, they set out on a world mission of invasions for plundering. The evolution of their economic system into **capitalism** impelled these newly formed merchants, pirates, and political thugs to scheme against the Church, the feudal lords, and each other in search of cheap labor, land, and natural resources. The whole point of this new system was to consolidate capital...so you could get more and more capital.

BUT WHAT IS 'CAPITALISM?'

"THE AFRICAN [SLAVE] TRADE WAS A VERY IMPORTANT FACTOR IN THE GROWTH OF THE CAPITALIST ECONOMY IN ENGLAND.... WITHOUT THE NEGRO SLAVE..IT IS UNLIKELY THAT... ENGLISH CAPITALISM COULD HAVE SHOWN THE PHENOMENAL GROWTH IT DID."
—W.E. WILLIAMS: *Africa & the Rise of Capitalism*

"THE [EUROPEAN] MEN OF THOSE DAYS WERE ACUTELY AWARE...THAT IT WAS AN AFRICAN PARTNERSHIP IN TRADE...THAT OPENED THE GATE TO NEW FORMS OF [EUROPEAN] ECONOMIC EXPANSION."
—BASIL DAVIDSON: *The Search for Africa*—1994

... AND WHAT IS 'CAPITAL?'

... AND HOW DOES IT ALL RELATE TO THE SLAVE TRADE?

Capitalism is an economic, political, and cultural system in which wealth—and the means of producing wealth—are owned and controlled by a small group of (*very rich*) people, whose ultimate aim is to get <u>more wealth</u> by any means at their disposal, even if it means stealing the fruit of another man's labor.

Capital is money used to generate more money. It has two forms: *Variable*—to buy labor power; and *Constant*—to buy the means of producing. The early European capitalists used African human beings as **capital.**

Enslaved Africans were not paid for their labor—they <u>were</u> labor. <u>And</u> they were a form of capital investment to generate more money (wealth).

WHAT DOES CAPITALISM HAVE TO DO WITH THE SLAVE TRADE?

There wouldn't have been any Slave Trade if it weren't for capitalism. The European slave trade became very profitable by the late 1600s. So much so, that in 1713 the Roman Catholic Church became a commercial go-between to stop European nations from fighting each other for access to the African coasts...and to boost the Vatican's wealth to obscene levels...including lots of prime land in the Americas. For a very generous fee, the Vatican created a contract (the *Asiento*) that resolved territorial and/or business disputes between two nations and thereby became

"THE PROFITS OBTAINED [FROM THE SLAVE TRADE] PROVIDED ONE OF THE MAIN STREAMS OF THAT ACCUMULATION OF CAPITAL IN ENGLAND WHICH FINANCED THE INDUSTRIAL REVOLUTION."
—C. ERIC WILLIAMS: *Capitalism and Slavery*

"MOREOVER, SLAVE-PRODUCED COTTON PLAYED A PIVOTAL ROLE IN THE EXPANSION OF...TRADE. THIS DIVISION...LAID THE BASIS FOR A NATIONAL [CAPITALIST] ECONOMY THAT EMERGED [IN THE U.S.] BETWEEN 1815 AND 1865."
—RONALD BAILEY

"...and remained for hundreds of years— the primary moral sanctioner for the brutal institution of slave trading."

—ASANTE & MATTSON: *Historical & Cultural Atlas of African Americans*

The slave trade was the driving force in the development of capitalism throughout Europe and the colonized Americas. For example:

 Between 1500 and 1750 the Slave Trade was the largest employer in Holland and Portugal.

 Barclay's Bank has its financial foundation set deep in the heart of the slave trade: its founders— David and Alexander Barclay established the bank in 1756 with the profits made in their slaving business.

 Lloyds of London, originally a coffee house, could not have become one of the biggest finance capital forces in the world without its legacy of dabbling in and insuring British slaveships and their cargoes.

"THE AFRICAN TRADE IS THE FIRST PRINCIPLE AND FOUNDATION OF ALL THE REST, THE MAINSPRING OF THE MACHINE WHICH SET EVERY WHEEL IN MOTION... THE AFRICAN TRADE IS SO VERY BENEFICIAL TO GREAT BRITAIN, SO ESSENTIALLY NECESSARY TO THE VERY BEING OF HER COLONIES, THAT WITHOUT IT NEITHER COULD WE FLOURISH NOR THEY LONG SUBSIST....
—MALACHI POSTLETHWAY, 18TH CENTURY CAPITALIST AND MERCANTILIST THEORETICIAN

The Watt's steam engine, the key technology of the Industrial Revolution, got its main financial backing from Caribbean slave owners funding inventor James Watt (whom he personally and publically thanked). One of the things that the Watt's Steam Engine did was to destroy the Indian and African weaving industries that had been producing high quality cloth for thousands of years... thus paving the way for cheap Britsh and Dutch cloth to be traded for Captive Africans, land, gold, spices, lumber, cheap Indian labor....

The demand for faster, bigger Slaveships was central to the European development of hydro-dynamics [17th & 18th centuries]: the science (and engineering) of moving objects through water with a minimum of energy.

The 18th century founders (Nicholas and Joseph Brown of Newport, Rhode Island) of Brown University got their wealth by manufacturing and selling slaveships as well as investing in the Slave Trade.

"THE FAMILY PATRIARCH, CAPTAIN JAMES BROWN [NO RELATION TO OUR "GODFATHER OF SOUL"), WAS THE FIRST PROVIDENCE MERCHANT TO ENTER 'THIS HAZARDOUS TRAFFIC' IN 1736. UPON HIS DEATH, HIS BROTHER OBADIAH AND FOUR SONS— JOHN, JOSEY, NICKEY AND MOSEY— WERE LEFT TO CARRY ON THE FAMILY SLAVE TRAFFIC... THE SHIP SALLY OWNED BY THE BROWNS AND CAPTAINED BY ESEK HOPKINS, SAILED TO THE COAST OF AFRICA IN 1764-65, AND AFTER NINE DIFFICULT MONTHS, SECURED 196 SLAVES. THE [AFRICAN CAPTIVES] REVOLTED AND A TOTAL OF 109 WERE KILLED, OR DIED FROM SUICIDES OR ILLNESS."
—RONALD BAILEY: *Agricultural History*

The Browns also received support from another merchant prince profiting heavily from the slave trade, Aaron Lopez— a Jew of Portuguese descent— who, like the Brown family, owned Slaveships and had other businesses directly related to the maintainance and development of the Slavery business. He was not the only formerly persecuted Jewish man deeply involved in the "Business." English-born Isaac Da Costa settled in Charleston, South Carolina, and by 1736 became not only the Lopez family hazzan (minister) but also their commission-merchant in the "Business." The 18th & 19 century New England Jewish petit borugeoisie played a key role in the rum distillation industry, particulary in Rhode Island. There were many Jewish businesses involved directly or indirectly with the Slave Trade— far more than were involved in the anti-slavery movement of the 18th and 19th century.

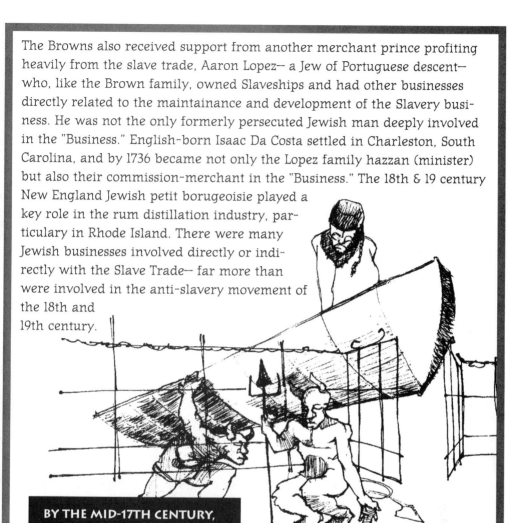

BY THE MID-17TH CENTURY, "JEWISH MERCHANTS BOUGHT A LARGE SHARE OF THE SLAVES TRANSPORTED BY THE DUTCH WEST INDIA COMPANY AND THEN RETAILED THEM TO THE PORTUGUESE PLANTERS ON CREDIT, AROUSING COMPLAINTS OF HIGH INTEREST RATES."
DAVID BRION DAVIS: "THE SLAVE TRADE AND THE JEWS" in *New York Review of Books*, DEC. 22, 1994

Aaron Lopez's biographer best sums up why persecuted Jews of the 18th century would engage in putting another People in such a savage bondage...

"How was it that such men could with such ease accommodate themselves to the revolting cruelties of the slave traffic? How is it that in all the letters which have been preserved and which relate to their interest in the [Slave] trade— and they [the Lopez Family] were for years active in this business— there is not one word of reproach, of doubt, of discomfort regarding the rectitude of chattel slavery? The answer is, of course, a sad commentary on human history. These men, in common with the great majority of their [white] contemporaries, simply never recognized Negro slavery for the scandal that it was. After all, even the Hazzan Touro gladly availed himself of a chance to supplement his meager income by sharing in the traffic.... To Aaron [Lopez] and his father-in-law, as to most [white] men in their day, Negroes were something less than human; leg irons and handcuffs were their natural habitat."

—**Stanley F. Chyet:** *Lopez of Newport.* 1970

Wall Street, in New York City, became a vital capitalist financial center because it was the first big slave trade center in the colonies and, later, the new nation's principal slave trading port, where the business of slavery was transacted (until 1862!).

And as the business of slavery went, so did all other businesses! For about 125 years, there was a *wall* that separated the financeers, speculators and bankers from the stench, humiliation and daily grime of young New York's vibrant slave trade business and African and white working-class residential areas.

Hence, the name Wall Street.

The slave trade and slavery were the economic basis of the French Revolution: 'The fortunes created at Bordeaux, at Nantes, by the slave trade, gave to the bourgeoisie that pride which needed liberty and contributed to human emancipation.' Nantes was the centre of the slave trade. As early as 1666, 108 ships went to the coast of Guinea and took on board 37,430 slaves, to total value of more than 37 million, giving the Nantes bourgeoisie 15-20% on their money.... Nearly all the industries which developed in France during the 18th Century had their origins in goods or commodities destined for the coast of Guinea or for America. The capital from the slave trade fertilized them; though the bourgeoisie traded in other things than slaves, upon the success or failure of the traffic everything else depended."

—CLR JAMES: *The Black Jacobins, 1963*

23

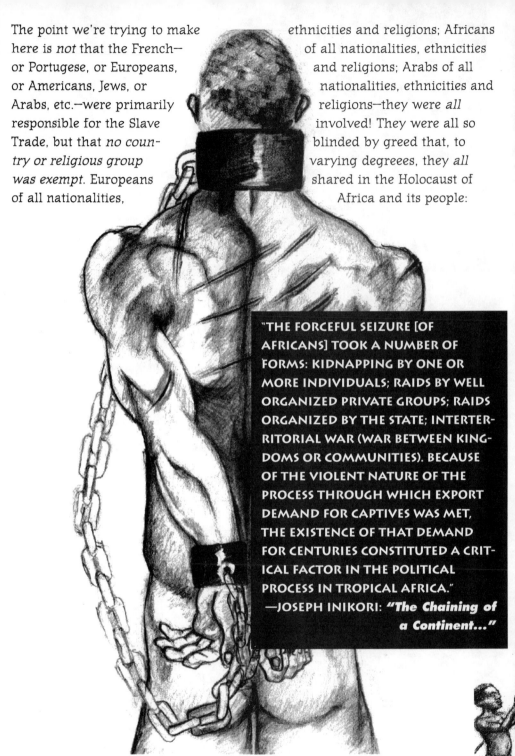

The point we're trying to make here is *not* that the French— or Portugese, or Europeans, or Americans, Jews, or Arabs, etc.—were primarily responsible for the Slave Trade, but that *no country or religious group was exempt*. Europeans of all nationalities, ethnicities and religions; Africans of all nationalities, ethnicities and religions; Arabs of all nationalities, ethnicities and religions—they were *all* involved! They were all so blinded by greed that, to varying degreees, they *all* shared in the Holocaust of Africa and its people:

"THE FORCEFUL SEIZURE [OF AFRICANS] TOOK A NUMBER OF FORMS: KIDNAPPING BY ONE OR MORE INDIVIDUALS; RAIDS BY WELL ORGANIZED PRIVATE GROUPS; RAIDS ORGANIZED BY THE STATE; INTERTER-RITORIAL WAR (WAR BETWEEN KING-DOMS OR COMMUNITIES). BECAUSE OF THE VIOLENT NATURE OF THE PROCESS THROUGH WHICH EXPORT DEMAND FOR CAPTIVES WAS MET, THE EXISTENCE OF THAT DEMAND FOR CENTURIES CONSTITUTED A CRIT-ICAL FACTOR IN THE POLITICAL PROCESS IN TROPICAL AFRICA."
—JOSEPH INIKORI: *"The Chaining of a Continent..."*

It is within this context that we *see* African societies growing and developing *before* the invasion of Western [i.e., Europe and the U.S.] capitalism. As a matter of ironical fact, **Africa gave birth to the Europe that would eventually rape and plunder it!**

CRADLES OF CIVILIZATION

Enlightened "liberal" Europeans have defined the "cradle of Civilization" as found between the Egyptian Empire and the early peoples of the Middle East (i.e., the Garden of Eden is supposedly located between the Tigris & Euphrates rivers in

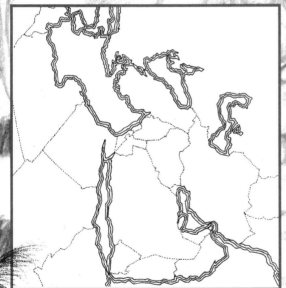

But the real deal is that there were *cradles* of African civilizations thousands of years before the creation of the vast empires of Egypt and Babylon that laid the foundations for the social, economic, technological, and spiritual bases for these great empires that eventually brought the gifts and powers to Europe through Greece and Italy.

The art of war, the martial arts, political economy and social classes for social control had their origin in African civilizations. Empires could not exist and survive for thousands of years without these fundamentals.

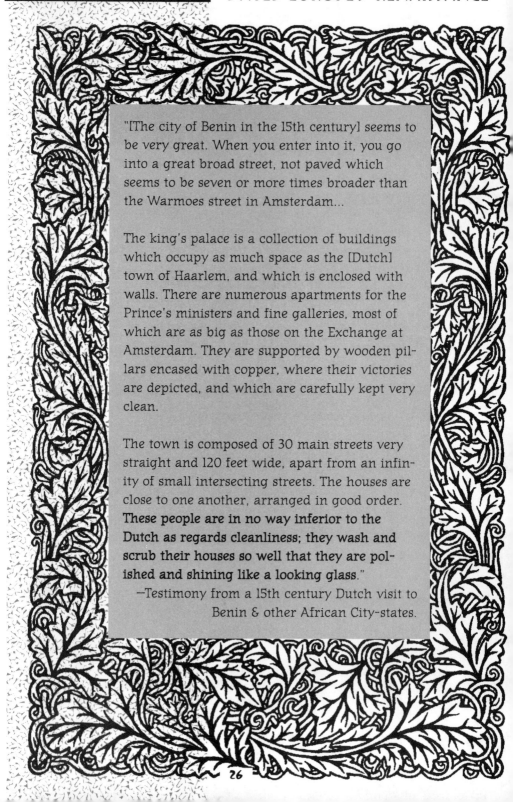

"[The city of Benin in the 15th century] seems to be very great. When you enter into it, you go into a great broad street, not paved which seems to be seven or more times broader than the Warmoes street in Amsterdam...

The king's palace is a collection of buildings which occupy as much space as the [Dutch] town of Haarlem, and which is enclosed with walls. There are numerous apartments for the Prince's ministers and fine galleries, most of which are as big as those on the Exchange at Amsterdam. They are supported by wooden pillars encased with copper, where their victories are depicted, and which are carefully kept very clean.

The town is composed of 30 main streets very straight and 120 feet wide, apart from an infinity of small intersecting streets. The houses are close to one another, arranged in good order. **These people are in no way inferior to the Dutch as regards cleanliness; they wash and scrub their houses so well that they are polished and shining like a looking glass."**

—Testimony from a 15th century Dutch visit to Benin & other African City-states.

It is very important that we assert this fact because it has been the duty of apologists for European culture to deny any connection to Africa, much less the existence of a *civilized* Africa before Europeans "discovered" it. The West has used the myth of white supremacy to justify its abuse of Africa and its descendants...

> "...IMPERIALISM, LIKE THE PREHISTORIC HUNTER, FIRST KILLED THE BEING SPIRITUALLY AND CULTURALLY, BEFORE TRYING TO ELIMINATE IT PHYSICALLY. THE NEGATION OF THE HISTORY AND INTELLECTUAL ACCOMPLISHMENTS OF BLACK AFRICANS WAS CULTURAL, MENTAL MURDER, WHICH PRECEDED AND PAVED THE WAY FOR THEIR GENOCIDE HERE AND THERE IN THE WORLD."
> —CHEIKH ANTA DIOP: *Civilization or Barbarism*

More specifically, the myth of white supremacy was used to justify the horrors of slavery; to continue to use Africans as capital so that European profits could grow and grow. And today it is used to recolonize Africa—*and* to justify why the U.S. *needs* more Black men in jail than in college.

AFRICA GAVE EUROPE THE FOUNDATION ON WHICH TO BUILD ITS CIVILIZATION.

"INSOFAR AS EGYPT IS THE DISTANT MOTHER OF WESTERN CULTURES AND SCIENCES... MOST OF THE IDEAS THAT WE CALL FOREIGN ARE OFTEN-TIMES NOTHING BUT MIXED UP, REVERSED, MODIFIED, ELABORATED IMAGES OF THE CREATIONS OF OUR AFRICAN ANCESTORS, SUCH AS JUDAISM, CHRISTIANITY, ISLAM, DIALECTICS, MECHANICAL ENGI-NEERING, ASTRONOMY, MEDICINE, LITERATURE (NOVEL, POETRY, DRAMA), ARCHITECTURE, THE ARTS, ETC.

JUST AS MODERN TECHNOLOGIES AND SCIENCES CAME FROM EUROPE, SO DID, IN ANTIQUITY, UNIVERSAL KNOWLEDGE STREAM FROM THE NILE VALLEY TO THE REST OF THE WORLD, PARTICULARLY TO GREECE, WHICH WOULD SERVE AS A LINK. CONSEQUENTLY, NO THOUGHT, NO IDEOLOGY IS...FOREIGN TO AFRICA, WHICH WAS THEIR BIRTHPLACE."
CHEIKH ANTA DIOP: *Civilization or Barbarism*

FACT At least half of the Greek language and Mythology is out of Africa by way of Egypt. (See Bernal's *Black Athena*.)

FACT Most of the great Greek architectural, sculptural, and mathematical ideas were either learned in Africa or taught to them by Africans. (For more documentation, detail, and proof see: **Diop's** *Civilization or Barbarism*.)

But how did all this change to African Enslavement.?

We must remind ourselves of the obvious: Africans were *not by nature* born to be slaves.
They were *forced* into it.

THE ORIGINS OF THE AFRICAN ENSLAVEMENT PROCESS

When the Egyptian empire began to crumble from internal rebellion by the oppressed majority and external confrontations with Greek, Roman, and various other forces from what we call the Middle East today, tens of thousands of people began to migrate south and west. They took with them the powerful knowledge that had developed within the 4000 year rule of the Egyptian Empire and merged this knowledge with that of the various societies they joined. That's why, for example, there are many words and ideas among the people who speak *Wolof* in West Africa that are so similar to words and ideas out of Ancient Egypt thousands of miles to the north, south, west and east.

For example:	
noh:	Egyptian and Wolof for 'the one who inflicts defeat'.
ba:	Soul, Vital Force in Egyptian.
ba:	Proper name in Wolof.
p(a)mer:	Pyramid in Egyptian.
Ba-meel:	Tomb, Tombstone in Wolof.
pa haw:	Grass in Egyptian.
ba-haw:	Grass in Wolof.
sity:	Proof in Egyptian.
seety:	to go verify in Wolof.

The Great Egyptian culture not only survived but it also spread across the African continent.

Even before the downfall of the Egyptian Empire, other African civilizations had been trading with Arabia and India and their cultures had begun to merge. (Today, for example, there are about 100 million identifiable "Africans"—called the **Dravidians** and the **Dasyu People** — living in southwestern India! The Ganges River was either named after a famous African hero or is a variation on the Arabic word for Black People: *Zanji.*)

Swahili is a language born out of hundreds of years of cultural, social, and economic interaction between Arab and East African peoples. The terms Zanj or Zanji and "Azania" originally were Arabic words meaning "African" (initially it meant nonEthiopian Africans) and "Land of the Black slave." But today, like "Black," "African," or "Third World," millions of Africa's oppressed sons & daughters have given "Azania" another more politically and racially positive meaning when they refer to a post-Apartheid South Africa as "Azania."

THE ARAB SLAVE TRADE

A change in the relationship between Arabs and east Africans began to set in around 650A.D.—a time when Europe was a Third World Country that would wait another 200 years before being introduced to civilization by the Moors of Africa.

(Europe, for all its arrogance, was one of the last places on earth to be civilized.) From 630 A.D. on, Muhammad's Army of Islam "unified" the peoples of the Arabian Peninsula, the Middle East, and much of Africa. Although the peoples of Arabia and the Middle East were sometimes "unified" by force, that was nothing compared to what befell the people of Africa—**the Arab Slave Trade**. The Arab slave trade lasted from the 652A.D. Arab-Nubian Slave Treaty until 1890 (it didn't truly end until 1911). Africans captured in wars by other Africans were sold into slavery for money or things (porcelin, silk and other fine fabric from the Asia) that powerful and corrupt African nobility desired.

Many of the enslaved Africans sold at the infamous Ujiji market were brought from regions far to the west of Lake Tanganyika...

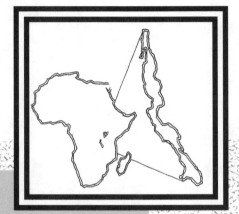

DURING THE CROSSING OF LAKE TANGANYIKA, THE SLAVES WERE MADE TO SIT DOUBLED UP IN THE BOTTOM OF CANOES, SO CLOSELY PACKED THAT BY THE TIME UJIJI WAS REACHED A QUARTER HAD SUCCUMBED, ALTHOUGH THE DISTANCE ACROSS THE LAKE... WAS SCARECELY 200 MILES....

NEAR THE SLAVE MARKET LAY AN UNCULTIVATED PIECE OF GROUND, THE CEMETERY, WHERE NOT ONLY THE DEAD, BUT THE DYING, TOO, WERE CAST. HYENAS, VERY NUMEROUS, GORGED ON HUMAN FLESH, AND WERE SO SATED THAT BODIES WERE LEFT HALF-DEVOURED.
—BEACHY: *The Slave Trade of Eastern Africa*

CASE: SLAVE TRADER, SAID BIN HABIB, IN THE MID-19TH CENTURY TOOK 300 SLAVES FROM THE TOWN OF MANYEMA, WEST OF LAKE TANGANYIKA. ONLY 50 ARRIVED ALIVE IN UNYANYEMBE.

Given the reality that the Muslim slave trade was 2 to 1 women (to fill the demand for concubines), we can reasonably assume that many of the leaders of the resistance movement among enslaved Africans were *women*. This gives us a new and different perspective on slavery and slave revolts: **it was not just about the destruction of African Manhood, it was also about the destruction of African Womanhood.**

"THE AVAILABILITY OF CON-CUBINES, MOREOVER, OFFERED A [MUSLIM] MAN A MEASURE OF RELIEF FROM THE UNHAPPINESS OF A MARRIAGE THAT WAS SEXU-ALLY UNGRATIFYING. BEFORE PURCHASING A SLAVE WHOM HE INTEND-ED TO USE AS A CONCU-BINE, A [MUSLIM] MAN WAS CAREFUL TO MAKE SURE THAT SHE WAS RESPONSIVE TO HIS ARMOROUS ADVANCES. THIS COULD BE MAN-AGED IN THE PRI-VACY OF SPECIAL STALLS THAT WERE SET ASIDE IN SLAVE MARKETS FOR THE CLOSE EXAMINATION OF FEMALE SLAVES BY PROSPECTIVE BUYERS; HERE MEN WOULD TAKE LIBERTIES WITH THESE HAPLESS GIRLS [12 TO 18 YEARS OLD!] IN A MANNER THEY WOULD NOT DREAM OF WHEN COURT-ING A [MUSLIM] WOMAN THEY WISHED TO MARRY...."
—Murray Gordon: *Slavery in the Arab World*. 1992

This lopsided enslavement process con-tributed to the depopulation of Africa by siphoning off potential and actual mothers of Africa. By the 17th century when the European slave trade had become the dominant process depopu-lating Africa, Africa's population growth remained stagnant for 200 years!

33

The rough census below gives the population in the millions:

	1650	1750	1850	1900
Africa	100	100	100	120
Europe	103	144	274	423
Asia	257	437	656	857

You will notice that both Europe and Asia roughly **quadrupled (400%)** in size during the 350 year period between 1650 and 1900. Yet, during the same period of time, Africa's population increased by only **twenty percent**. *(See page 155 for the real significance of those numbers.)*

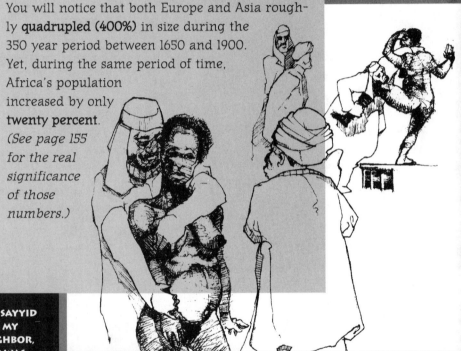

Let us be clear: It was the *Arabs* who set the foundations for exporting Africans, for taking the people of Africa to strange and horrible lands. But Africans were not considered "capital" by the Arabs as they were by capitalists. It was true that many Arabs saw Africans as inferior human beings destined for bondage. And lots of money was made capturing, preparing, selling and buying Africans. But this was done within the tributary economic framework. And many of the Arabs were *themselves* Africans! Take, for example, this reference to the famous South Arabian poet al-Sayyid al-Himyari (723–89):

34

Arab literature was strewn with negative, even racist, references to dark skinned Africans:

The blacks do not earn their pay by good deeds, and are not of good repute
The children of a stinking Nubian black—
God put no light in their complexion!

This was written by an Arab poet during the late 600A.D. satirizing the African governor of Sistan in 671A.D.; but ironically, it *also* referred to Ubaydallah— the son of *Abu Bakra*, one of the African companions of the Prophet Muhammad, the spiritual head of *all* Arabs who was apparently not blinded by the racism that afflicted many of his followers.

Sharaf al-Zaman Tahir Marvazi makes it clear that "blackness" by 1120A.D. in parts of the Arab World connoted negativity: "blackness, though a defect, has its use in some instances; such as...when the government agents dress in black in order to inspire the subjects with awe and fear."

There are very few societies that don't consider rape as part of the privilege of conquest (or one of the *tools* of conquest). The Arabs were no exception. They considered women inferior to men and raped African women, with all the humiliation that implies.

By the same token, Arab men often married African women and allowed some of them to become part of the royal families as equals. That's why you'll find hundreds of thousands of "African-featured" people throughout Asia Minor (the Middle East) today.

In the Arab world an enslaved African could become free, if he/she worked off their price. And their children—in general—were *not* enslaved.

HOW DID AFRICANS BECOME ENSLAVED?

The Arabs took advantage of regional wars in Africa to buy captives from the victor. They also used the old divide-and-conquer technique. They worked one group against the other and took or killed the best and strongest. The Arabs eventually (especially from the 1400's onward, with the help of the ruthless Portuguese) began to raid the coastal towns (Mombassa in Kenya, Kilwa, Sofala, Mogadishu...) and also ventured hundreds of miles inland to what we today call Uganda, Malawi, Rwanda, and Burundi to capture Africans who were peacefully minding there own business...

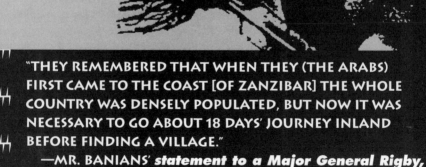

"THEY REMEMBERED THAT WHEN THEY (THE ARABS) FIRST CAME TO THE COAST [OF ZANZIBAR] THE WHOLE COUNTRY WAS DENSELY POPULATED, BUT NOW IT WAS NECESSARY TO GO ABOUT 18 DAYS' JOURNEY INLAND BEFORE FINDING A VILLAGE."
—MR. BANIANS' *statement to a Major General Rigby,*
ca. 1875-6

THE AGHAS:

THE CENTRALITY OF EUNUCHS IN MUSLIM SOCIETY

Castrated male slaves—Aghas or eunuchs—were central to familial peace, protection and order in many wealthy Muslim households. Eunuchs were considered so valuable that they sold for almost ten times more than non-castrated male slaves—African *or* European. In spite of their high price, eunuchs (popularly referred to as *"khadim"* or *teacher* or *tutor*) were seen by the hundreds of thousands in many parts of Muslim society.

Eventually, the "craft" or "surgery" became the profitable hallmarks of Coptic priests throughout Upper Egypt, the Sudan, and Ethiopia.. They would amputate the scrotum and penis of 8-to-12-year-old African boys so completely that it was called "levelling with the abdomen." Over the hundreds of years and hundreds and thousands of "operations," the survival rate ranged from one in ten to one in thirty. The young boys of Burkina Faso were the most sought after because of the extreme poverty and orphaned children due to the constant attacks upon their people. But they also came from Darfur, Kordofan, Dongola, and towns in Ethiopia [earlier known as Abyssinia].

"THE NEED TO PROCURE EUNUCHS OUTSIDE MUSLIM LANDS SPRANG FROM THE REQUIREMENTS OF ISLAMIC LAW. THIS VERY LAW WHICH FORBADE MUSLIMS FROM REDUCING [ANOTHER MUSLIM] TO SLAVERY UNDERSTANDABLY BARRED THEM FROM MAKING HIM INTO A EUNUCH.... ISLAMIC LAW, IN ADDITION, PROHIBITED MUSLIMS FROM PERFORMING THE OPERATION; AND, AS A RESULT, CASTRATING YOUNG BOYS [8 TO 12 YEARS OLD] BECAME A TASK THAT FELL TO NON-BELIEVERS, TO BE DONE IN THEIR OWN COUNTRY. THE UNENDING STREAM OF DESEXED BOYS WHO WERE WALKED OR TRANSPORTED BY BOAT OR CARAVAN FROM THEIR NATIVE LANDS IN EUROPE AND LATER AFRICA [BECAUSE AFRICAN BOYS' SURVIVAL RATE WAS HIGHER AND THERE WERE MORE OF THEM] ARRIVED READY MADE IN MUSLIM COUNTRIES."
—GORDON MURRAY: *Slavery In The Arab World*

Imagine the trauma, pain, screams, infections, confusion of little African boys crying for their mother, father, brothers, sisters, grandmother...somebody to come and rescue them from this nightmare. And, if you survived, imagine growing into manhood with confused sexual urgings that had to be sublimated into busy details of the daily life of your Masters' women, his business, his political affairs...

In contrast, white boys were actually *quasi*-eunuchs because the castration process was only cutting the tip of the penis and leaving the scrotum intact. Most were able to have sex and a few were even allowed to have wives and concubines!

The beastly act of castrating African boys was a part of Muslim slavery from as early as the 900s A.D. Thus, for a thousand years, hundreds of thousands of African *Aghas* were castrated; this impacted not only upon them , but upon the men and women they served.

Centuries of enslaving Africans left the Arab trader a cold and hollow person who, either through natural birthright or centuries of intermarriage, often was of African descent himself. Even so, he and his cohorts saw the enslaved African as no more than a sex-slave or a two-legged oxen or cow: cheap beasts of burden or pleasure...and there were plenty more where they came from...

CONCUBINAGE AND THE HARIM [HAREM] MADE WOMEN INTO A FOCAL POINT OF THE MUSLIM SLAVE TRADE. THEIR DIFFERENT USES AS DOMESTIC, MISTRESS, AND SEX OBJECT ASSURED A CONTINUOUS DEMAND FOR YOUNG FEMALE SLAVES. IN THESE MULTIPLE ROLES THEY STRENGTHENED THE PATRIARCHAL FAMILY, WHICH IS AT THE BASIS OF MUSLIM SOCIETY. THE MERGER OF THIS FORM OF SLAVERY INTO THE STRUCTURE OF FAMILY LIFE HELPED MAKE SLAVERY INTO A FORMIDABLE INSTITUTION IN THE ISLAMIC WORLD AND SAYS MUCH ABOUT WHY IT BECAME SO DIFFICULT TO DO AWAY WITH IT.
—MURRAY GORDON: *Slavery In The Arab World*

In the mid-1800s, the Arab slave trade was bringing $5 to $17.50 for healthy adult and $2 to $6 for a healthy child. But a donkey would cost between $11.50 and $30! There were more battles going on between Africans, thus more captives to be sold than ever before. Thus, eventually by the mid-19th century, enslaved Africans sold for 50¢ a head. Some Europeans and Arabs even traded a cow for 5 Africans or a donkey for 6 Africans.

THE RAIDS AND CARAVANS OF CAPTIVES

The Arab slavers would go inland and raid at nightfall, just as the villagers were having their communal dinner. Those who resisted or tried to run away were shot. When the Arabs encountered more warlike Africans, they used the divide-and-conquer method. The Arabs would stir up conflict between two groups, then lend their support to one group over the other. The African victors traded their captives for Arab trinkets: beads and cloth.

The Arab caravans of enslaved Africans grew. The Arabs would kill most of the adult men because they had resisted and would most likely continue to resist; their deaths served to put fear in the hearts of the living. The slavers would take enough captives so that a good number would survive for selling. They were then divided into smaller, more manageable groups which set out on different routes back to the coast. The captives were forced-marched all over the countryside as the Arab slaver gathered more captives. Young men, women, and children of all ages were bound by hand (either with hemp or leather which grew tighter as time went on) and by neck yokes to each other and forced to walk for hundreds of miles through dense forests, savannas, mountains, and waterways. If they got sick, they were left behind...*often still bound or yoked to another sick or dead person.* To make matters worse, they were constantly whipped and *all* — men, women and children— were treated as beasts of burden, carrying loads of ivory and other African treasures. In the 1200 years of Arab slavery, tens of millions of Africans died before they could even be sold.

Slavery was so institutionalized on the East Coast of Africa that one Tanganyikan coastal town was called *Bagamoyo*:

"Here we leave our souls."

In fact, *Bagamoyo* was one of the most important slave embarkment ports for those captives destined for Zanzibar—the Arab slave trade's key island. Over the seven centuries (from 900 to the 1600s A.D.) of the early Arab slave trade, hundreds of thousands of Africans died crossing the Indian Ocean between Tanganyika, Kenya, and Zanzibar. Arab slave ships carried 200 to 400 captured Africans jammed together, either on an open deck or below the deck with no regard for sex or age, for sanitation or food quality. The trip could take one day to reach Zanzibar or it could take two weeks. Either way, there was not enough food and no health support. So the loss of African lives averaged about half of the original human cargo.

Numbers?

It's impossible to certain, but according to our best estimates: At least 9.64 million African women and 4.75 million African men were sold in the Arab Slave Trade.

Some **14 to 20 million** African men, women, and children were killed either trying to resist capture, en route to be sold, waiting to board the slave ships or caravans bound for the Muslim world, at the holding pens and dungeons...or in the process of being castrated for eunuch slavedom.

Africans must be a powerful people to have survived all that.

But this was just the beginning of the misery and the test of survival.

PART 2: THE EUROPEAN SLAVE TRADE: THE EYEWITNESS ACCOUNTS

To begin with, the European Slave Trade, was not *trade* at all...

THE PROCESS BY WHICH CAPTIVES WERE OBTAINED ON AFRICAN SOIL WAS NOT TRADE AT ALL. IT WAS THROUGH WARFARE, TRICKERY, BANDITRY AND KIDNAPPING. WHEN ONE TRIES TO MEASURE THE EFFECT OF EUROPEAN SLAVE TRADING ON THE AFRICAN CONTINENT, IT IS VERY ESSENTIAL TO REALISE THAT ONE IS MEASURING THE EFFECT OF SOCIAL VIOLENCE RATHER THAN TRADE IN ANY NORMAL SENSE OF THE WORD.

—WALTER RODNEY: *How Europe Underdeveloped Africa*

THERE WAS NO WAY TO KNOW IT THEN, BUT THEIR CREWS OF MEN AND BOYS CAME FROM MANY PORTS AND MANY PASTS TO FIND THE SHORES OF AFRICA. THEY SAILED FROM AMSTERDAM AND LISBON, FROM NANTES AND LA ROCHELLE, FROM BRISTOL AND LONDON (AND LATER...) FROM NEWPORT AND BOSTON AND NEW YORK ON SHIPS WITH STRANGE NAMES. THEY CAME TO US ON <u>BROTHERHOOD</u> AND <u>JOHN THE BAPTIST</u>, ON <u>JUSTICE AND INTEGRITY</u>, ON <u>GIFT OF GOD</u> AND <u>LIBERTY</u>; THEY CAME ON THE GOOD SHIP <u>JESUS</u>. BUT BY THE TIME OUR WEARY LINES OF CHAINED AND MOURNING TRAVELERS SAW THE VESSELS RIDING ON THE COASTAL WAVES, THERE COULD BE BUT ONE NAME. ONE MEANING; CAPTIVITY. THUS IT WAS ON THE EDGE OF OUR CONTINENT— THE REALITY OF THE LAND—THAT THE LONG STRUGGLE FOR BLACK FREEDOM BEGAN.

—VINCENT HARDING. *There Is a River*

As with the Arab slave trade, thousands upon thousands of West and Central Africans were captured during wars between rival African kingdoms and traded with the European slaver for trinkets (beads, cloth, liquor, guns, foodstuff...).

Many West African states came into existence primarily for war: Kong, Bobo Dioulasso, Segu, Sikasso.... Slave trading and slave raiding were central to these states. Their respective leadership would have to pay tribute to their chief architect of this slave-based centralized kingdom—the *Damel Lat Sukaabe*, the king of the Wolof Kajor Empire from 1695 to 1720. All these states and others throughout West Africa, as far south as Angola and as far north as today's Senegal, were Slave Warrior-based states during the 200+ years of the 17th, 18th, and 19th centuries. During this period, Africa had witnessed the creation of **ten generations** of Warrior Slaves; **ten generations** of brutal male dominance over African women; **ten generations** of corrupted, greedy, and immoral local and regional aristocracy; **ten generations** of farming and training

for the development of the European slave trade ... the foundation for West African dependency, depopulation, and underdevelopment.

The result was a fundamental change in the culture and spirit of the people. Where there was once a spirit of cooperative work and shared responsibilty, each village, clan, town, or state looked out for itself by any means necessary—often at the expense of others.

The result: over the centuries, hundreds of thousands of African men and women were captured to be the warrior servants of powerful local rulers who, in turn, were loyal civil and economic servants of the king (or queen) who ruled these centralized states. The enslaved women were used to serve the needs of the Warrior Slave: cooking, washing, farming and sexual pleasures. The enslaved men were trained to be fierce and fearless raiders of villages and towns, to capture and wreak havoc. Hiding or trying to rationalize their killing and plundering ways, these Warrior Slaves were loud talking, brightly and fancifully dressed boisterous boozers who lived for the moment. (Sound familar?)

44

In the Wolof Kingdom alone, these Warrior Slaves amounted to at least 100,000 annually. In fact, there were always more Warrior-Slaves than the Captives they took to be sold to the Europeans. Four to five million of these Warrior-Slaves and their female companions died over this very same 200+ year period. Yet, these men and their attendant enslaved women are never counted in the Black Holocaust numbers!

As the Europeans demanded more and more Captives, many of these African states became not only traders in human beings, but also the main providers (merchants and transporters) of the foodstuff for the MiddlePassage and the holdover slave dungeons.

It takes a lot of food, organized farming, and distribution to feed thousands of people a day over regions as vast as thousands of square miles. Yams, rice, corn, cassava, collard greens, fruits, cattle, sheep, chickens, pigs, etc. had to be cultivated, stored and/or cured, shipped and distributed. Prices had to be constantly negotiated between all involved parties— including the enslaved farmer.

THE CHANGEOVER TO WARLIKE ACTIVITIES AND KIDNAPPING MUST HAVE AFFECTED ALL BRANCHES OF ECONOMIC ACTIVITY, AND AGRICULTURE IN PARTICULAR. OCCASIONALLY, IN CERTAIN LOCALITIES FOOD PRODUCTION WAS INCREASED TO PROVIDE SUPPLIES FOR SLAVE-SHIPS, BUT THE OVERALL CONSEQUENCE OF SLAVING ON AGRICULTURAL ACTIVITIES IN WESTERN, EASTERN AND CENTRAL AFRICA WERE NEGATIVE. LABOUR WAS DRAWN OFF FROM AGRICULTURE AND CONDITIONS BECAME UNSETTLED. DAHOMEY, WHICH IN THE 16TH CENTURY WAS KNOWN FOR EXPORTING FOOD TO PARTS OF WHAT IS NOW TOGO, WAS SUFFERING FROM FAMINES IN THE 19TH CENTURY.
—WALTER RODNEY: *How Europe Underveloped Africa*

Records show that hundreds of thousands of Africans enslaved by their fellow Africans over the centuries of European slave trade were able to buy their way out of slavery and smoothly integrate into their former slaving society. It typically took West African enslaved farmers about five years of hard work and good harvesting to buy out of slavery.

Moreover, we see in this redirecting of agricultural techniques and traditions the beginning of the process of *underdeveloping* Africa for the sake of *developing* Europe and Euro-America. This *undervelopment* process would become the Black Holocaust's fundamental long-term devastation of all of Africa.

FAMINE

Suddenly, farming was about cash crops for the slave trade. West African farmers were no longer farming in a balanced way to help replenish soil nutrients and stop erosion. The result was that the 18th century brought some of the worst famines in West African history. It got so bad that free Africans sold themselves or their children into slavery to buy food. During the 1757-58 famine in the Senegambian region, a French commander released 500 enslaved Africans because there was not enough food to keep them alive within the castle-fortress. (You can be sure that he looked forward to recapturing them when conditions improved.)

The famine of the 18th century was not the result of drought, locusts, or any other natural disaster—it resulted from the disintegration of traditional methods of dealing with the ups and downs of nature. When the Warrior Slaves invaded, they ransacked the graineries and other storages, forcing the survivors— older men and women, the disabled, little children— into the hills or barren land where it was impossible for them to survive.

The European

The Eyewitness Accounts

By the late 1600s, European slave traders had become the scourge of Africa. They would travel up key rivers like the Gambia or the Congo and raid villages and whole kingdoms. They would overwhelm the villagers with their cannons and rifles. They would, as they had learned from the Arab slavers, attack at dinner time or just before sunrise. They would set fire to parts of a village and force men, women, and children to run from fear of being burned to death, into their own captivity.

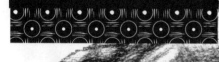

Slave Trade

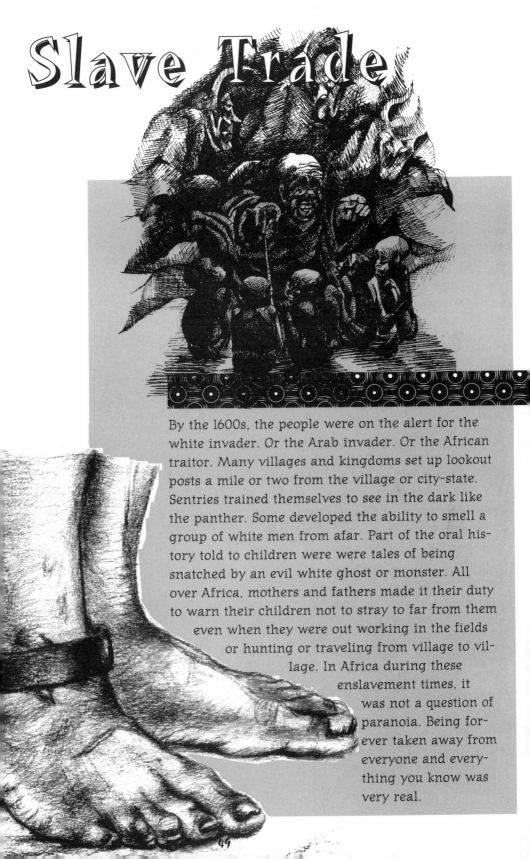

By the 1600s, the people were on the alert for the white invader. Or the Arab invader. Or the African traitor. Many villages and kingdoms set up lookout posts a mile or two from the village or city-state. Sentries trained themselves to see in the dark like the panther. Some developed the ability to smell a group of white men from afar. Part of the oral history told to children were were tales of being snatched by an evil white ghost or monster. All over Africa, mothers and fathers made it their duty to warn their children not to stray to far from them even when they were out working in the fields or hunting or traveling from village to village. In Africa during these enslavement times, it was not a question of paranoia. Being forever taken away from everyone and everything you know was very real.

"With an assortment of sundry goods amounting to about 1400 pounds sterling, it may be reasonably expected to get about 300 slaves or more, which brings them to near the rate of 5 pounds a head."

--Slaver James Barbot: c.1700

not trained as a warrior (young boys and girls were trained in the martial arts in many African societies), you were supposed to either hide or try to sneak back to the town or village and warn others of the invaders. Often, this meant children having to watch as their mother or father or sister or brother or uncle or aunt or cousin was dragged off or shot trying to run away from the slave catchers.

Suddenly, your family is ripped apart. You may— and this happened often— be only five or six years old and successfully hid yourself from the white invaders and their black partners only to find out that you are all alone or stranded with another child. There are stories of children walking miles, days, nights, determined to find somebody—*anybody*—friends, relatives, or a new village to join. Because adults knew that a time might come when they would be separated from their children, many taught their three-year-old children what to eat in the bush or rainforest; how to use the sun and stars for direction, and how to walk quietly through any terrain. For the child it was just a game.

Until the day, without warning, the game became survival...

"One day, when only I and my dear sister were left behind to mind the house [in the kingdom of Benin], two men and a woman got over our walls, and in a momemnt seized us both.... They stopped our mouths and ran off with us into the nearest wood... The next day proved a day of great sorrow... for my sister and I were separated while we lay clasped [weeping] in each other's arms...

I cried and grieved continually, and for several days I did not eat anything but what was forced into my mouth...."
—Olaudah Equiano: The Interesting Narrative of the Life of Olaudah Equiano (Equiano was 11 years old at the time of his capture.)

" Here a most sorrowful scene imaginable to be witnessed!— Women, some with four, or six children slinging to their arms, with the infants on their backs, and such baggage as they could carry on their heads, running as they could through prickly shrubs... while they were endeavouring to disentangle themselves...they were overtaken and caught by the enemies with a noose of rope thrown over the neck of every individual, to be led in the manner of goats tied together, under the drove of one man.

I was thus caught— with my mother, two sisters (one an infant about 10 months old), and a cousin. The last view I had of my father was when he came from the fight [against the enslavers], to give us the signal to flee..."
—Samuel Ajayi Crowther—14 years old—of Oyo, Nigeria. 1821

If you were caught in one of these raids (there were thousands of raids every year all over Africa— particularly West Africa), and you were a woman, you would most likely be sexually abused. Rape, public and private, gang and individual, was a primary form of *disempower-ing* a powerful and proud people. It was usually the first act after all were rounded up and shackled and yoked. African men shackled, yoked, held at gunpoint, could only look on as their mother, daughter, sister, wife, relative, friend were put through some of the most degrading acts a human could do to another. Children were sexually violated in the most brutal ways, often leaving them bleeding to death or racked with trauma...not to mention syphilis or gonorrhea. For the white men— often poor illiterate outcasts, Christianity and their male-dominated culture had so distorted sexuality, that the madness of rape and sexual abuse was looked upon as a reward, as proof of their "manhood," as evidence that they at least had power over some thing: *The African.* And this made them loyal to "the Company" which paid them not only with cash but with sex, booze, and a semblance of power.

For the women of Africa to be attacked, it was never a question of age, looks, size, or what shade of brown you were. If you were one of the fortunate ones not raped or sexually abused, you were still beaten, shackeled, and deprived of any privacy. The violence was consciously intended to announce that you were no longer in control of any part of your life for the rest of your life and the lives of your children now and to come.

All this was happening, and you hadn't even arrived at the coastal European forts!

Thus, the conditioning (some slave traders called it "seasoning") process was immediate and relentless. The goal of the European was to deliver to the slaveship a beaten people, a docile people, a person who saw herself or himself as something less than human. Many Captives did give up on the long trek to the coast and became passive and part of the living dead. They had seen and experienced brutality, torture, and unspeakable sexual attacks on men, women—even children—beyond their imagination and concluded that these white men were evil superhumans destined to keep them forever in tortuous bondage. The captured African woman could never look at slavery or the white man without feeling the experience of being violated. As a way of surviving, many women removed their souls from what their flesh was experiencing. They dug deep into themselves and became outwardly whatever the white man desired.

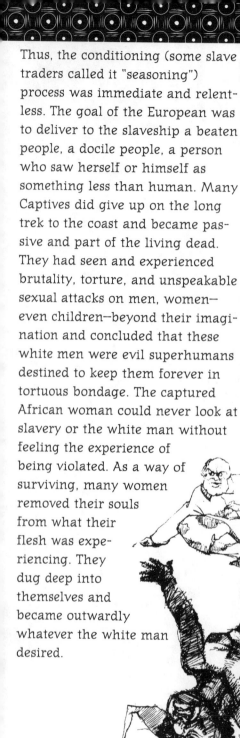

Nealee started out but she couldn't or wouldn't make it. She was being driven to the West African coast for sale when she became ill and refused to walk another step. Mungo Park, who was one of the last persons to see Nealee, said she was put on an ass "but the ass was so very unruly, that no sort of treatment could induce him to proceed with his load; and as Nealee made no exertion to prevent herself from falling, she was quickly thrown off, and had one of her legs much bruised. Every attempt to carry her forward being thus found ineffectual, the general cry of the coffle [slave caravan] was, kang-tegi, kang-tegi, 'cut her throat, cut her throat: an operation I did not wish to see performed, and therefore marched onwards with the foremost of the coffle. I had not walked above a mile when one of Karfa's [the leader's] domestic slaves came upon me, with poor Nealee's garment upon the end of his bow and exclaimed, 'Nealee affeeleeta.' (Nealee is lost.) I asked him whether the Slattees had given him the garment as a reward for cutting her throat; he replied that Karfa and the school-master would not consent to that measure, but had left her on the road, where undoubtedly she soon perished, and was probably devoured by wild beasts."

—Bennett: *Before The Mayflower*

There were a few who felt submission and collaboration would be a way to survive and avoid public humiliation. But they had a rude awakening to the permanency of slavery: no matter how you try to please your captor, there is no freedom at the end. So these women got deeper into self-hate and hatred of their African selves and people. They acted white. They looked down upon the African women who were forced to stay in the waiting dungeons and factories (shacks into which the slavers packed Africans). These self-hating women had washing privileges for offering sexual favors to the Masters. They were sexually violated so often that these African women did not live more than a year. You see, they too were put on the slaveship and had to continue their "favors" usually for the whole white crew at any time and any place.

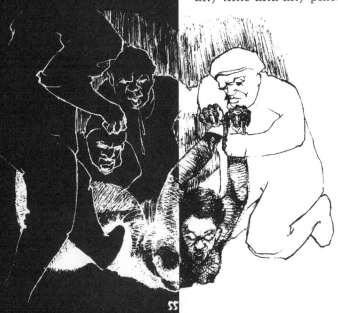

make one's skin feel very slimy or exude a horrible odor. They would pass these herbs among those loyal to the cause of Freedom for protection. Sometimes, women who knew the European language would use their sexuality to gather information about where the caravan of enslaved Africans was heading or about the weaknesses of the invader's army.

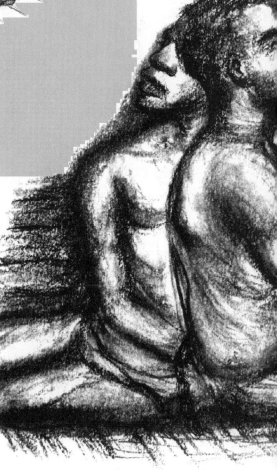

The majority of Captive women found ways— often ingenious— of not only surviving but resisting the dehumanization of slavery. They were the ones who soothed others' pains of loss and violence. They were the ones who found ways to get nutrition from the plants around them to help all to survive. They were the ones— in spite of chains on the ankles and hands— who found ways to help the pregnant and sickly (the slaver would leave you to die if you were thought to be sick. Nobody wanted to buy a sick worker with whom you have *to put out money* before you could *make money*). On the trek down to the coast, some of the women would look for herbs that would, for example, in an attempted rape cause a man's private parts to burn for hours. Or, use herbs that would

Often a caravan would not make it to the port town. Captives would be able to organize to the level of distracting a few of the guards, killing them, taking their weapons and begin the process of overunning the rest...often, all the while still shackled! If successful, most would try to return home and rebuild their community. A few would be so moved by their experiences that they would travel the countryside, warning and telling others of their encounter with the white slaver. These stories are today still part of many West and Central African societies' oral traditions.

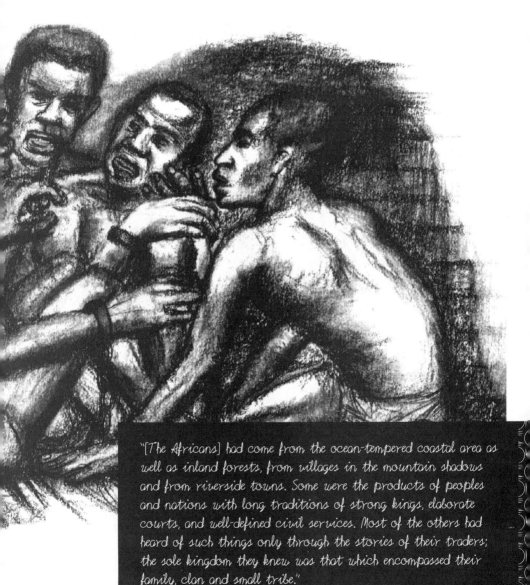

"[The Africans] had come from the ocean-tempered coastal area as well as inland forests, from villages in the mountain shadows and from riverside towns. Some were the products of peoples and nations with long traditions of strong kings, elaborate courts, and well-defined civil services. Most of the others had heard of such things only through the stories of their traders; the sole kingdom they knew was that which encompassed their family, clan and small tribe."

—Harding: *There is A River*

The Conditions in these Slave Castles

"their prayers and song for freedom must have filled the air like a bittersweet dust."

—Harding: There Is A River

Once the surviving captured Africans arrived at the coastal town, they could smell death and degradation. The slave ports were the most unsanitary of towns. The captured Africans were corralled either into tiny shacks known as *baracoons* or *factories*. Among the Captives were African artists and artisans—miners, blacksmiths, potters, weavers—now jammed into damp, cramped cells. Farmers, priests, musicians, each indistinguishable from the other, herded like animals into dank cells to wait...to wait...

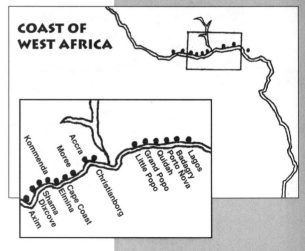

COAST OF WEST AFRICA

Kommenda
Accra
Moree
Cape Coast
Christianborg
Grand Popo
Porto Nova
Quidah
Little Popo
Lagos
Badagry
Shama
Elmina
Dixcove
Axim

Branding Africans with the slave company's emblem or numbers were common over the tens of thousands of days of the slave trade. This often caused severe infections among our ancestors. Infections that lead to fevers, pain so severe that men and women would pass out or scream themselves to sleep. For some, the infection spread and became gangrene, forcing the Europeans to cut off their limbs or to kill the African outright. Afterall, he or she would be no good to a slavemaster with one arm or leg. But even worse, these infections would spread throughout a hole or section of the castle and create deaths and weakened captured Africans.

The infection would spread to pregnant women who would become so ill that they would be forced to abort. Sometimes the abortion was induced by the use of herbs they smuggled with them from their villages. Most of the time they would have to "dispense" with the fetus without the sanitary care or ceremony so central to their spiritual well-being.

n addition, alcoholism
became a critical illness
among the corrupted
African elite:

No slave trader could afford
to dispense with a cargo of
rum.... The Negro deals were
plied with it, were induced to
drink till they lost their rea-
son, and then the bargain was
struck. One [18th Century
African] slave dealer, his bag
full of the gold paid him for
his slaves, stupidly accepted
the slave captain's invitation
to dinner. He was made drunk
and awoke the next morning to
find his money gone and himself
stripped, branded and enslaved
with his own victims, to the
great mirth of the sailors."
—Eric Williams: Capitalism &
Slavery. 1944.

The Captives would stay two to four weeks— or sometimes months— waiting to be shipped out to the Americas or Europe. Sometimes, thousands would stay for months because of political or economic struggles within the newly developing European nations and/or colonies. Or they would remain in these hell-holes while European rivals would fight for control of that region of the slave trade. Remember: the Europeans built castle-forts for two reasons: to fight off invasions from fed up Africans—and to fight other Europeans. Often African Captives would stay for months on end because the Slaveships were waiting for still more Captives to arrive in the port town. No "good" slaveship Captain would leave Africa without a full (or overfull) ship.

These baracoons or factories were shacks so small that an adult could hardly stand up in them. Usually dirt-floored without windows and a door, they would house 30 to 50 Africans (of the same sex) within a 10 foot by 15 foot floorspace. The temperature inside was well over 90 during the day and night.

These hot and humid conditions meant that the Captives were always perspiring and living within an environment conducive to various forms of disease.

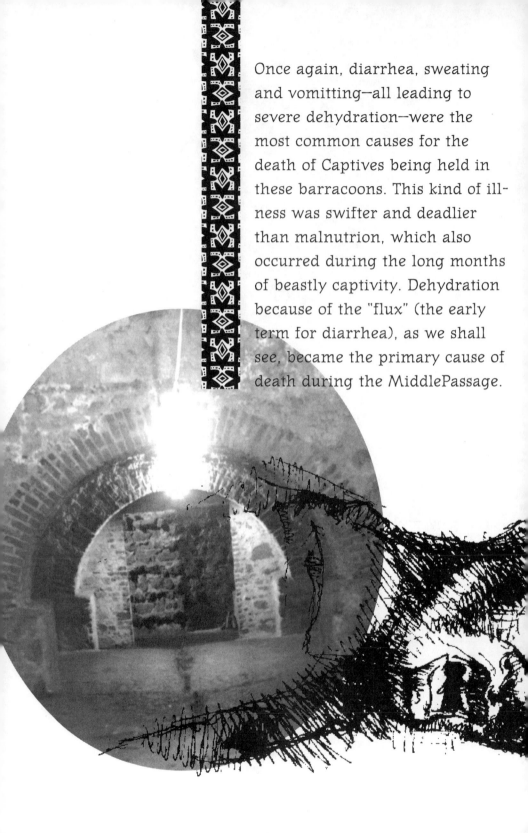

Once again, diarrhea, sweating and vomitting—all leading to severe dehydration—were the most common causes for the death of Captives being held in these barracoons. This kind of illness was swifter and deadlier than malnutrion, which also occurred during the long months of beastly captivity. Dehydration because of the "flux" (the early term for diarrhea), as we shall see, became the primary cause of death during the MiddlePassage.

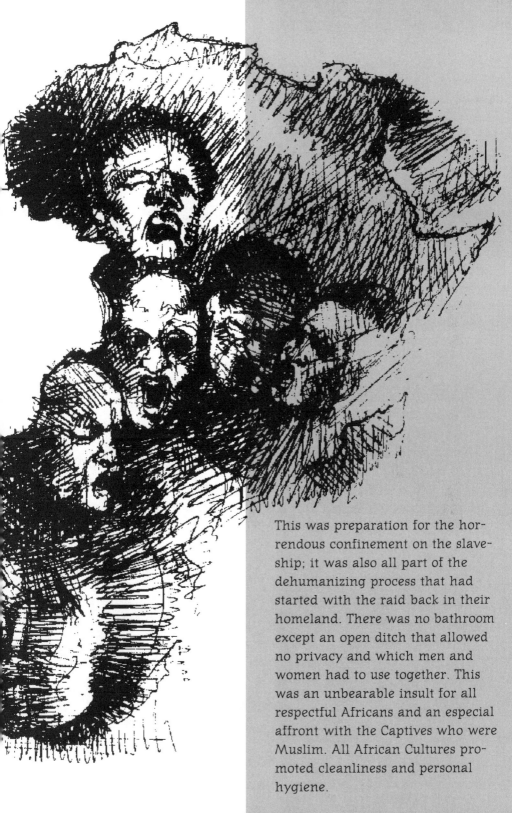

This was preparation for the horrendous confinement on the slaveship; it was also all part of the dehumanizing process that had started with the raid back in their homeland. There was no bathroom except an open ditch that allowed no privacy and which men and women had to use together. This was an unbearable insult for all respectful Africans and an especial affront with the Captives who were Muslim. All African Cultures promoted cleanliness and personal hygiene.

The inability to bathe daily and for women to hygenically care for their menstruation added insult to injury, further forcing many Captive Africans into depression. Many could not bear the ever-present stench. They would constantly be sick. Unable to eat, sleep or freely move about. Many would either try to commit suicide, bicker and fight with others, run away, or just snap and start screaming or silently rocking with dead faces. Many of those would waste away, only to be thrown out to the edge of town by the slavers and left to die. The vultures other animals would begin eating them while they were still alive. In some cases, the slaver, finding no potential money in them, would shoot them or club them to death in full sight of other Captives. This was a warning to the healthier African Captives: If you get sick or fake it, your fate is death.

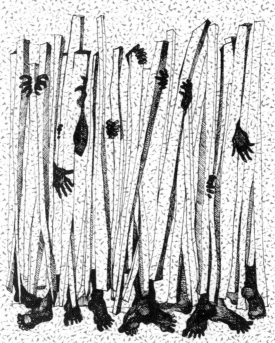

The everpresent stench came not only from unwashed African and European bodies, open sewers, and filthy shanties, but also from the rotten food served the Captive Africans. This food—either poorly preserved vegetables and meats set aside for the Captives, or leftovers of the white enforcers—was thrown into a pile outside of the barracoons and subsequently passed on to the Africans as their one meal for the day. Some European slavers were "liberal" and fed their Captives twice a day.

This "food" was a mush of boiled vegetables: yams, collard greens, or other vegetables native to the region. In certain coastal towns, it included rice. Rarely were they fed meat or fish. If they were, it was saltfish or salted beef or pork (an insult, perhaps intentional, to the Muslim Captives). On a few occasions, plaintian or other tropical fruits were served. The African Captives were allowed a pint of water at the time of their meal— if no drought prevailed...or if the slaver was not trying to save a few pennies by not serving water— which often happened during the dry season.

On Negotiating The Selling of African Captives

"Negotiations were often protracted. Prices and exchanges fluctuated greatly; traders, Africans, clients, local chiefs and their retinues, all had to be satisfied. Nor was it simply a matter of agreeing [on] a price. [Slave-trading on the coast developed it own conventions, rituals and etiquette, all of which had to be observed. Gifts were offered and accepted, drinks and smokes exchanged, food cooked and consumed together..... Sometime violence and bloodshed terminated proceedings. Generally, however, at the point of contact between black and white, the slave trade was a well established routine with its own protracted code of conduct which provided the essentiual lubricant for a potentially abrasive commerce."
—James Walvin: *Black Ivory*– 1992.

Once the paperwork, money and trading trinkets were transacted between the African slave catchers or local corrupt chiefs and the European company and/or government officials, the captured Africans were then marched into the Fortresses' dungeons.

"The lodgins and apartments within the castle are very large and well-built of brick, having three fronts, which, with the platform, on the south, almost make a quadrangle, answering to the inside of the walls, and form a very handsome place-of-arms well paved, under which is a spacious mansion [a massive airless dungeon!— S. E. Anderson], or a place to keep the slaves in, cut out of the rocky ground, arched and divided into several rooms; so that it will conveniently conatin a thousand Blacks, let down at an openeing made for the purpose. The keeping of the slaves thus underground is a good security against any insurrection.
[A round tower constructed on top of an adjecaent rock hosed six 12-pound cannons] which serves to keep the Blacks in the town in better awe, as well as to defend them from all other Blacks their enemies."
—Cape Coats Castle in 1682 as described by Jean Barbot

These fortresses were called castles because they were not only military structures, they were also offices *and* living quarters for the European traders and government officials. The vast majority of them were located along the coast of what we call Ghana, Nigeria, The Ivory Coast, Benin, Togo and The Gambia today. In fact, between the 16th and 19th centuries 36 of the 48 major enslavement castles were within this region formerly called by the European slavers and traders as the Upper Guinea Coast (with smaller regional names such as the **Slave Coast, the Gold Coast... The Ivory Coast**). They were massive structures built out of the cliffs or hillsides on or very close to the Atlantic Ocean. Deep within them were the tiny dark, damp, smelly, rat infested, lice-ridden raw holes in which the captured Africans were "processed" and kept. For example, one of the oldest slave fortresses is the **Elmina** Castle (in present-day Ghana) built in 1482 by the Portuguese and not taken over by the British until almost two centuries later around 1665. Another, **Cape Coast** Castle, initially built by the Swedes in 1653 was seized by the rulers of the Fetu people was "acquired" by the Dutch in 1664 and then "acquired" by the British the following year. Castles like **Cape Coast, Goree** or **Elmina** could hold hundreds to more than 1000 captured Africans in some of the most horrible conditions ever experienced by humanity.

"Above all else the slave castles and forts came to epitomize the value and apparent permance of the slave trade.... They were buildings which spoke of the confidence of the [European] men and the trading companies which built them. They were, however, rooted in an economic philosphy which was slowly disintegrating..."
—James Walvin: Black Ivory—

NOTE: These were fortresses of white men. No European women were allowed into these centers of human trade and misery (until the 19th century) to check out— at their leisure— the African women below being allowed outside for exercise and a washdown.

For the African woman there was no privacy. At anytime of the day or night, the captain or businessman or commander could sit and select the woman or women or girls he would choose to rape. If you refused, you were whipped and then raped. And if you were really resistant, there would be a gang rape often leading to death or insanity. In addition, the rape and sexual abuse of African men and boys would also be a frequent occurrence. You can be sure that, over the tens of thousands of days and nights of the Slave trade, no demented sexual fantasy was left untried upon the bodies and souls of the African Captive.

The Particular Trauma of the Enslaved African Woman

Facing a strange and hostile environment in North America, "African females undoubtedly experienced great emotional and physical distress. Yet, their anguish and alienation did not begin on the coast of the 'New World.' For several weeks and sometimes months before they ever reached North America, African girls and women suffered incredibly at the hands of the [slave] traders, European and African, who captured or bought them. Torn from the very fabric of their lives, these women, many of whom were already married and had children of their own, were forced to leave their families, their culture, and their ethnically prescribed identities behind.... They were sold along with the other regional 'treasures' for which different areas of the West African coatline were named— gold, ivory, and grain."
—**Brenda E. Stevenson,** "Slavery;" in *Black Women In America*, Vol. II. 1994

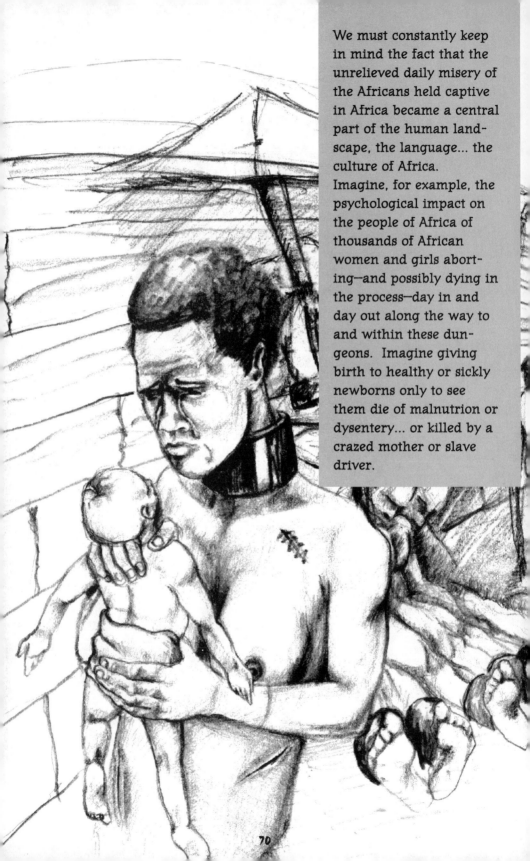

We must constantly keep in mind the fact that the unrelieved daily misery of the Africans held captive in Africa became a central part of the human landscape, the language... the culture of Africa.

Imagine, for example, the psychological impact on the people of Africa of thousands of African women and girls aborting—and possibly dying in the process—day in and day out along the way to and within these dungeons. Imagine giving birth to healthy or sickly newborns only to see them die of malnutrion or dysentery... or killed by a crazed mother or slave driver.

It's no wonder that Europeans involved in the "Trade" at any level, had to justify the beastial violence and squalid conditions inflicted upon their fellow human beings. By the late 1500's European "scientists," intellectuals and priests began to make popular the notion of Africans as subhumans and uncivilized beasts of burden being "saved" by slavery. (The Chinese Ruling Lords had used a similar obscene strategy some 500 years earlier in refence to their enslaved East Africans.)

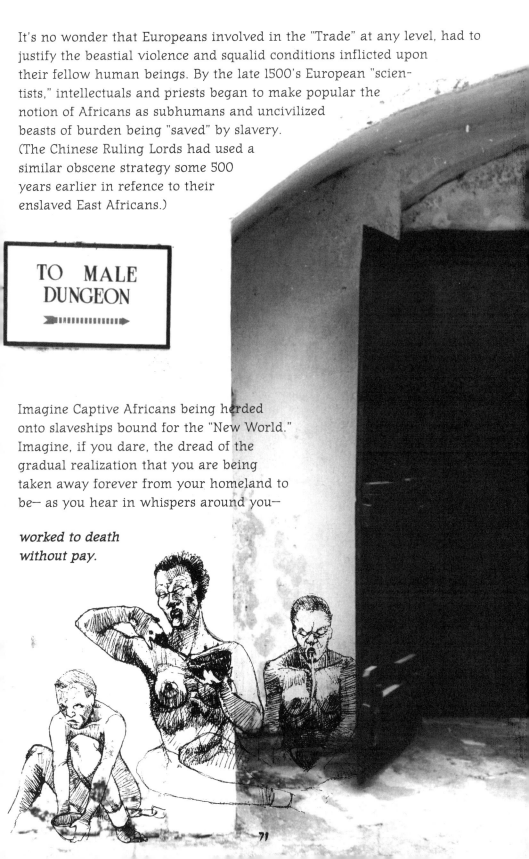

TO MALE DUNGEON
▶▪▪▪▪▪▪▪▪▪▪▪▪▶

Imagine Captive Africans being herded onto slaveships bound for the "New World." Imagine, if you dare, the dread of the gradual realization that you are being taken away forever from your homeland to be— as you hear in whispers around you—

worked to death
without pay.

By the time the people of Africa were herded into the slave castles, many were not only stripped of their clothes and jewelry but also stripped of their minds, spirit, culture. Many felt humiliated, betrayed by their own countrymen...betrayed even by their Gods. These captured Africans, chained inside the slave castles, either submitted to enslavement and Christianity with the feeling that there was nothing they could do about it or looked for ways, either literally or spiritually, to commit suicide.

The vast majority of the enslaved, however, saw the need to fight for their freedom and were part of the Resistance Movement... the African Liberation Struggle:

"As is so often the case with human struggles for liberation,
the first stages of the baracoon-based movements toward
Black Freedom required internal action, exertions of the
will. In many places it was probably necessary to break
through all the real and fancied barriers of each particular
geographic, tribal and national history represented in these
first confused and unlikely pan-African assemblies. For
within the flexible matrix of our continental oneness, over
the long millennia of the ages, Africa has produced great
diversity. Even in the relatively limited setting of the western portions of the continent; which supplied most of the
men, women and children who filled these prison spaces,
there was a fascinating, compelling variety of human experience.... As they identified themselves to one another and
spoke their names in those dark prison places, the sounds
of their tribes and nations must have tumbled like a water-
fall out of the river of the past: Bambara, Malinka, Fon,

...For struggle was inevitable. Reflection on the great and
varied African past was not sufficient. Now all these histo-
ries were jammed into one frightening present, and it was
evident that they were being rushed forward into a new
history, one which had no real precedent in the countless
centuries of our past (except for the Moslems among us
who told their stories of the Captive people who followed a
certain Moses). So by the time the ships arrived, there
could no longer be any doubt that we had been captured in
our homeland to prepare us for a greater, uncharted, whol-
ly terrifying captivity across the endless waters...."
                                    —Harding: *There Is A River*

PART 3:

SLAVESHIPS & THE MIDDLEPASSAGE

"...we stood in arms, firing on the revolted slaves, of whom we kill'd some and wounded many... and many of the most mutinous leapt over board, and drowned them- selves in the ocean with much resolution...."
—John Barbot: Slaveship Captain, 1702

The actual transition of the Captive African from dungeon to ship became more bureaucratic as the centuries of slavery rolled on. Initially, in the 1400s, the Europeans just forced the survivors of their raids onto their ships with minimal food for a month at sea. But when large corporate con- cerns, the Catholic Church, and the State became involved, there were many hands to grease and a small avalanche of paperwork. Given that the basis of slavery was capitalism and at capital- ism's heart was good old-fashioned greed, these partners in the crime of slavery each had elabo- rate schemes to rip each other off.

By the late 1600s, the European slave trade was no longer an easy *run-in-and-raid* operation for a swashbuckling few. It was capitalism's first big multinational business, with all of its varied political and economic policies that promote and protect the "business." It had to payoff corrupt African rulers and terrorize those who resisted the "business." It had to justify the "business" with the Bible and "the-need-to-civilize-them" propaganda. It had to expand the "business" throughout Africa and, in the process, steal more and more land to help maximize the profits... or die!

Make no mistake: Capitalism cut its teeth on the blood of the people of Africa; so there is no escaping the fact that every fabric of Western society is linked to that blood, to those atrocities, to the millions upon millions of African dead that the West is yet to acknowledge. No part of the West is left untouched: science, technology, culture, religion, economics...politics all were (and are) twisted to feed the insatiable greed of capitalism.

The "Triangular Slave Trade" —

Myth or Historical Reality?

Contemporary apologists and "rationalizers" for slavery still assert that there was **not** an ongoing organic link between the development of the U.S. capitalist economy, Caribbean slavery and Africa or Europe. Many of these mythmaking "historians" have rewritten history to downplay or deny Western capitalist development as being directly dependent upon the enslavement of Africans and the slave trade. Fortunately, there is an abundance of documentation proving that Colonial and Post-Colonial America was not just an intimate partner in a triangular trade based on enslaved African labor, but was directly linked to a "polygonal" trade involving England and many other European countries... and Asia (primarily India and China)!

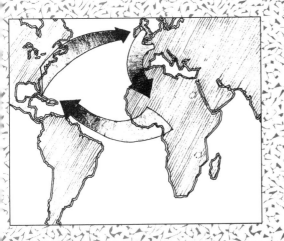

MOST RHODE ISLAND SLAVING VOYAGES ORIGINATED AT ONE OF TWO PRINCIPAL PORTS [NEWPORT AND BRISTOL] AND CONFORMED TO THE TRIANGULAR PATTERN LONG ASSOCIATED WITH BOTH THE ENGLISH AND THE AMERICAN SLAVE TRADE.... THE TRADE ASSUMED ITS CLASSIC THREE-POINT CONFIGURATION ALMOST FROM THE OUTSET.... A SECOND LEG OR 'MIDDLE PASSAGE' WAS PROBABLY ADDED TO THE ITINERARY IN THE 1730'S, IF NOT SOONER. MOST OF THESE SO-CALLED SLAVES WERE EXCHANGED FOR SPECIE, BILLS, AND RETURN CARGOES OF SUGAR OR MOLASSES.

—J. COUGHTRY: *The Notorious Triangle*

A TOTAL OF 523 (OUT OF 934) RHODE ISLAND SLAVING SHIPS WERE IDENTIFIED BY DESTINATION OR SLAVE MARKET [DURING THE EARLY TO MID 1700'S]. THESE SHIPS CARRIED SLAVES TO MORE THAN 40 'NEW WORLD' PORTS, BUT NEARLY 2/3 OF THE SLAVES WERE SOLD IN THE WEST INDIES AND 31% IN VARIOUS MAINLAND NORTH AMERICAN MARKETS. COUGHTRY'S WORK ENABLES US TO PUT ONE MATTER [THE EXISTENCE OF THE TRIANGULAR TRADE] TO REST...

—RONALD BAILEY: "SLAVE TRADE AND...CAPITALISM IN THE U.S."

Goods Traded in the British Triangular Slave Trade

Wool: A British product that had little practical use in tropical Africa became a "prestigous" item demanded by corrupted African elites.

Cotton: "What the building of ships for the transport of [Captive Africans] did for 18th Century Liverpool, the manufacture of cotton goods for the purchase of [Captive Africans] did for 18th Century Manchester." —Eric Williams

Refined Sugar: The British created an industry that took the crude brown sugar that was cut and initially processed by enslaved Africans in the Caribbean and processed it in England.

Distilled Rum: Rum comes from the distilliation of molasses (a by-product of molasses). African slaves would separate and store the molasses in barrels to be shipped to England (and the US). "Rum was indispensible in the fisheries and the fur trade, and as a naval ration. But its connection with the triangular trade was more direct still. Rum was an essential part of the cargo of the slave ship, particularly the colonial American slave ship. No slave trader could afford to dispense with a cargo of rum. It was profitable to spread a taste for liquor on the [African] coast." —Eric Williams

The Metallurgical Industries: The slave trade demanded tens of thousands of guns, iron chains, cuffs, yokes, makes, padlocks and branding irons. "According to tradition, ships sailed to Africa with holds full of idols and manelloes [brass bracelets], while the cabins were occupied by missionaries—'an edifying example of a material good in competition with an immaterial one.'" —Eric Willims

Brass wires—along with thousands of tons of copper sheathing—were used for the slave ships...

THE SLAVESHIP: IT'S NOT A CRUISE LINER

"[The enslaved Africans] were all enclosed under grated hatchways, between decks. The space was so low that they sat between each others' legs, and stowed so close together, that there was no possibility of lying down, or at all changing their position, by night or by day... . they were all branded like sheep, with the owners' marks of different forms. These were impressed under their breasts, or on their arms, and as the mate informed me with perfect indifference, burnt with a red hot iron...."

—a Mr. Walsh—a British passenger on the Slaveship North Star

"The good ships" *Jesus, the Gift of God, the Liberty, the Justice, the Black Boy, the Brotherhood, the African Glory, Africa...* and hundreds of others from the Arab Kingdoms, Sweden, Holland, France, Spain, Portugal, England and the United States were nothing but floating dungeons. For the enslaved African, these scribblings on the bow of the ships were translating into even more misery and death. For them it meant going from one kind of stench to another, more ferocious kind. Boarding these floating hellholes meant Freedom thru Death.

THE HORRORS OF

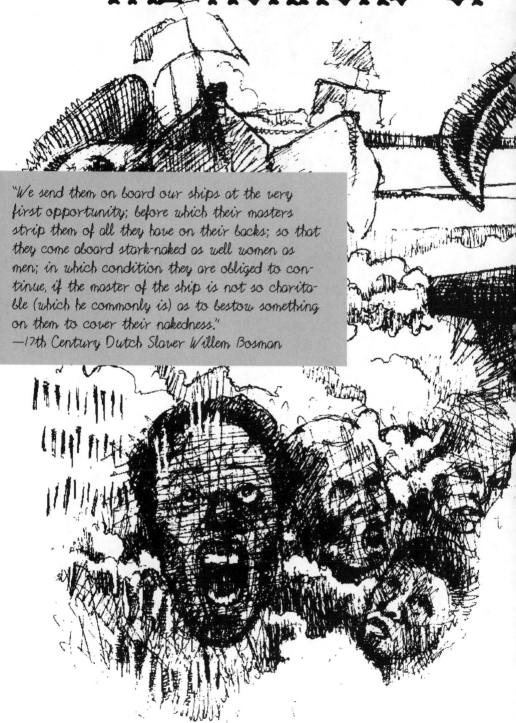

"We send them on board our ships at the very first opportunity; before which their masters strip them of all they have on their backs; so that they come aboard stark-naked as well women as men; in which condition they are obliged to continue, if the master of the ship is not so charitable (which he commonly is) as to bestow something on them to cover their nakedness."
—17th Century Dutch Slaver Willem Bosman

THE MIDDLEPASSAGE

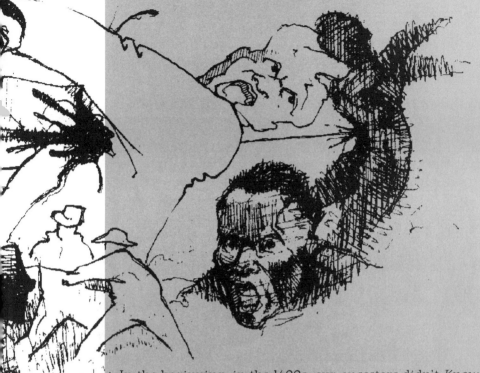

In the beginning, in the 1400s, our ancestors didn't *Know*....
But by the 1500s they *Knew*. They knew that to walk that
gangplank naked with hands and feet shackled meant facing
some things that were far worse than death. Some tried to
jump into the dangerous waters around the piers. Some
tried to turn around and run back to the Land. Many wept.
Tears of fear, anger, hatred, humiliation, frustration... long-
ing for Home and Family.

Still others had expressionless faces because they had
already been "broken" or "seasoned." They had accepted the
imposed status of "Negro slave": a semiperson with no land,
no roots, no culture, no selfdetermination... no freedom.
"Negro": an empty black vessel for the whims of white folks.
Before they even boarded the Slaveship, they had already
been stripped of their African names and given meaningless
and degrading "European" names like Tim, Black Mary,
Johnnyboy, Bessie, Jamima (for Amina or Halima), Cuffy (for
Kofi), Cudjoe (for Kwadjo), Quashee (for Kwesi), Tom, Scipio,
Raphael, Lucia, Lucy.

AFRICAN RESITANCE CONTINUES...

Captain Tomba was first seen in a slave pen in Sierra Leone. John Atkins, a [British] surgeon who saw him there said he was a handsome man "who scorned looking at us, refusing to rise or stretch his limbs, as the Master commanded." A few days later Captain Tomba and a companion led a revolt on a slave ship and killed three sailors before they were subdued.

What happened to Captain Tomba?

"Why," John Atkins wrote, "Captain Harding weighing the Stoutness and Worth of the two slaves [Captain Tomba and a companion] did, as in other Countries they do by Rogues of Dignity, whip and scarify them only; while three others, Abettors, but not Actors, nor of Strength for it, he sentenced to cruel Deaths; making them first eat the Heart and Liver of one of them killed. The Woman he hoisted up by the Thumbs, whipp'd, and slashed her with Knives, before the other Slaves till she died."

—**Lerone Bennett:** *Before the Mayflower*

There were many— hundreds, thousands— who were thinking as they boarded the floating torture chambers. Thinking. Scheming about how to insurrect. How to get back Home. How to break the white-man's neck or smash his skull with a cannonball. They were the Kofis, the Afuas, the Captain Tombas, the Cinques, the Azingas, the Nandis, the Abduls and Aminas, the Chakas, the Dedans of the ever-present resistance movement during the MiddlePassage. These were the men and women who were **organizers** and **spiritual advisors,** whispering to the others to... *"keep holdin' on. I've got a plan..."* Sometimes that message would have to go through four or five different translations—but everyone who needed it, got it.

NOTE—
The Captive Africans who were forced to the Americas came from throughout the entire African Continent, but the vast majority came from about 110 ethnic groups.

83

Resistance, insurrection, rebellion, revolt... revenge by any means possible... was the order of the day every day for the Enslaved Africans. They were inventive, resourceful, well-organized, and passionately determined to be free:

"[the organized African Captives] had pieces of iron they had torn off our forecastle door, as having premeditated a revolt, and... they had also broken off the shackles from several of their companions feet... as well as all other things they could lay their hands on, which they imagined might be of use for their enterprise. Thus armed, they fell in crowds and parcels on our men, upon the deck unawares, and stabb'd one of the stoutest of us all, who received fourteen or fifteen wounds of their knives, and so expir'd. Next they assaulted our boastwain, and cut one of his legs so round the bone, that he could not move... others cut our cook's throat to the pipe, and others wounded three of the sailors, and threw one of them overboard...

[Eventually] we stood in arms, firing on the revolted slaves of whom we kill'd some, and wounded many: which so terrified the rest, that they gave way, dispersing themselves...between decks, and under forecastle; and many of the most mutinous, leapt over board, and drowned themselves in the ocean with much resolution, showing no manner of concern for life."

—Slaveship Don Carlos's captain's log: 1702

"Wednesday, April 12, 1843— It was a strange scene which presented itself to us when we mounted her [Slaveship Cleopatra] side. The deck was crowded to the utmost with naked negroes, to the number, as stated in her papers, of 450, in almost riotous confusion, having revolted, before our arrival, against their late masters; who,

Captain John Newton, a deeply "Christian" man, was ordained in 1754 into the Church of England (which condoned and profited from slavery). While transporting hundreds of Captive Africans on one of his Deathships, Captain Newton penned one of the most famous of all hymns—"Amazing Grace." It is ironic that "Amazing Grace" has become a staple of African American sacred music (i.e,. Gospel), often sung with great feeling at funerals. Many people have thought it to be an African American song! (Maybe Captain Newton heard a mournful melody emanating from the Africans he had brutalized in the slave-deck below him.)

on their part, also showed strong excitement, from feelings, it may be supposed, of no pleasant nature. The negroes, a meagre, famished looking throng, having broken through all control, had seized everything to which they had a fancy in the vessel; some with hands full of 'farihna,' the powdered root of the mandioc or cassava; others with large pieces of pork and beef.... Many more were busily dipping rags, fastened to bits of string, into the water-casks".

—Pascoe G. Hill: Fifty Days On Board a Slave-Vessel. 1848

THE AMISTAD MUTINY: 1839

One of the most significant African revolts on board a slaveship took place on June 28, 1839 near Cuba:

In April of 1839, the son of a prosperous Mende (West Africa) rice farmer was kidnapped and sold to Spanish slave merchants who, upon arrival in Havana, placed Cinque (sometimes referred to as Joseph Cinquez)—the son of a prosperous *Mende* rice farmer—on board the *Amistad* (how ironic that this ship is called "Friendship") that was destined for Puerto Principe, Cuba.

However, Brother Cinque and the 50 other African Captives had other plans: They meant to take over the ship and return to Africa. They successfully killed the captain (a Mr. Raymon Ferrer) and the cook and so frightened some of the Spanish sailors that they jumped ship and attempted to swim ashore. Since Cinque and his African bretheren did not know how to steer a European built ship, they had to rely upon the Spanish owners— Jos_ Ruiz and Pedro Montez—to guide them back to Africa. Even though they were tied to the bridge, the Spaniards steered the ship toward the US instead of Africa. They did this by steering southwestward (toward Africa) during the day and northeastward (toward America) during the night.

For two months, the Spaniards zigzagged them up the US coast. During that time, the Africans lost 10 of their comrades to dehydration and starvation. On August 20th, Brothers Cinque, Carlee, Dammah, Baah, Monat, Nahguis, Quato, Con, Fajanah, Berrie, Gabbo, Fouleaa, Kimbo, Faquannah, and Connia went ashore at Culloden Point to get water and other provisions.

The US Navy *Washington crew* spotted the ship off the coast of Montauk Point, Long Isalnd, New York while Cinque and 14 of his men were on shore. Lt. Gedney and an armed militia boarded the *Amistad* (anchored a half mile from shore), saw that it was under the control of Africans, and immediately arrested them as runaway slaves. The Africans— except for 3 girls under 12— were charged with murder and mutiny and held in New Haven and Hartford (Connecticut) jails.

Fortunately for Cinque and his African comrades, the trial was set in the "liberal" antislavery city of New Haven. There was sympathy and support from the white abolitionists. But the most important and critical support came from the African communities of Connecticut and New York. Black solidarity was so strong that James Covey, an enslaved *Mende* sailor based in New Haven, volunteered to translate for Cinque during the trial.

"When the trial began, Cinque testified in his own behalf. From his carriage and countenance, everyone could see that he was a man of considerable natural intelligence and diginity. He handled his testimony with deftness and eloquence. [John] Covey... translated Cinque's words quickly, without hesitation. The [United States Circuit] Court ruled in favor of the Africans. However, the decision was appealed to the Supreme Court. Former President John Quincy Adams was emotionally moved by the plight of the Africans and undertook to argue their case before the Supreme Court....

On March 9. 1841, President John Quincy Adams argued for eight-and-a-half hours [before the Supreme Court] in support of [Cinque and his fellow Africans]. The Africans were freed."
—M.K. Asante & M.T. Mattson: *Historical & Cultural Atlas of African Americans*

Antonio, the enslaved African who was the property of Spain, was returned to the Spanish as their property as per US-Spain treaty agreement. He was the only survivor of the Amistad Rebellion who was re-enslaved.

This Supreme Court decision and the Dred Scott Decision sixteen years later (March 6, 1857) were crucial, highly publicized and politicized legal battles in the struggle to end US slavery. The progressive leadership of both free and enslaved African communites in the US used these Supreme Court decisions to mobilize their brothers & sisters into a united force for Freedom. The victory of Cinque and his companions also helped solidify the Black *and* white abolitionist movements in the Northeast, thereby helping "persuade" the US governement to forcibly act on ending slavery in the south and their newly seized territories of the Midwest.

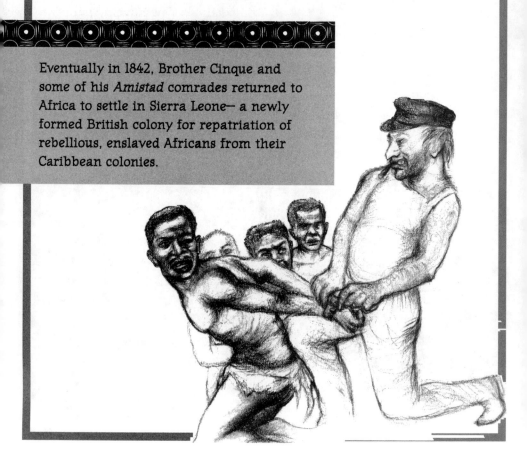

Eventually in 1842, Brother Cinque and some of his *Amistad* comrades returned to Africa to settle in Sierra Leone— a newly formed British colony for repatriation of rebellious, enslaved Africans from their Caribbean colonies.

DEMENTED SEXUALITY

As the naked African Captives were boarding the ship, the captain or his crew would likely be looking over which men or women, boys or girls, they were going to sexually molest during the voyage:.

"On board some ships, the common sailor was allowed to have intercourse with such of the black women whose consent [!?] they can procure. The offices are permitted to indulge their passions among them at pleasure, and sometimes are guilty of such brutal excesses, as disgrace human nature."
—Alexander Falconbridge— Slaveship surgeon: 1789.

"The officers had all provided themselves with three or four wives [what a twist of words!] each, and rebuked me for not bringing mine along, alledging that they would... bring a good price when we arrived in America."
—Slaver Joseph Hawkins: 1793.

One must remember, that since these "good Christians" saw Africans as sub- or semi-humans, there would be no moral crime committed through rape. In fact, they did not perceive of it as rape. It was "keeping the morale high." Or "diversion from boredom."

64

Of course, some white men blamed *their* sexual attractions toward African women/girls (and men/boys) on the Africans! The Africans' nudity— which of course had been *forced upon them by their morally upstanding white captors*—was projected onto the Africans as a plot to seduce morally upstanding white men (who rarely— if ever— saw a naked *white* woman). So, the Africans were blamed for the twisted desires of their white captors... forcing Antiguan slavemaster John Singleton to write "poetically" (in 1702)...

Shun the false lure of Ethiopic charms
Wherein consists their beauty or their grace?
Perhaps the dark complexion of the slave
The eye enjoys, and in an aspect foul
Wanton delights, entraptur'd to behold
deformity of features, shape and soul;
Detested composition! made more vile
By th'unsightly fashion of their garbs:
Or does the sable miss then please you most,
when from her tender delicate embrace
A frouzy fragrance all around she fumes?
Can such intice? For Shame!, the vice reform...

The fact that slave owner Singleton's poetic plea was largely ignored is attested to by the million shades of Brown one can see all over the Americas and Africa today...the result, over- whelmingly, of the white rapes of African women.

THE DEATHSPIRIT

Even given the fact that Europeans were enslaving the people of Africa, it is *still* hard to imagine why the Europeans designed the Death Ships—and the Slave Decks inside them—in a way that compounded the torture: The Captive Africans—*our Ancestors*—had to squeeze through narrow stair-wells (more like holes) into the two, three, or four decks below. The smell of death was every-where. It was in the wood and tar of the ship's hull. It was in the creaky masts and the dingy canvas sails. The nasty hemp nets slashed to the sides of the ship to catch Africans who would choose death in the Atlantic or Indian Oceans rather than remain enslaved.

The people of Africa, like the people of many cultures, believed that the Spirits of the Dead move among the living. So, on those Death Ships, spiritually sensitive Africans felt, saw, heard— *experienced*—the trapped Spirits of the Dead Ones. The Europeans did not sense these essences and did not believe in anything like African Ghosts (European Ghosts, yes! *But Nigga Ghosts?* Preposterous!). So when they saw an African man or woman react to these Spirits, in their eyes they were just some frightened crazy African who's scared of their own shadow. But the other Africans *Knew*. And *understood*.

Even when the slaveship was new, our ancestors felt the Deathspirit and sang out a warning that needed no translation...

SLAVE EXIT TO
AWAITING BOATS

PART 4

THE DEATH SHIPS

the Narrative

New or old, slaveships were designed to maximize the number of human cargo. A slaveship's capacity would range from 120 to 1000 Captives or more. The "average capacity" was about 400 Captives— whether it was a Dutch, North American, British, Spanish, Portugues, or French slaveship. We will never know the true numbers because it was normal for the captain to pack more Captives than the ship was registered for. He would "work the books" so that his personal slave booty would make it to the Scramble or Auction Block— be they five or fifty extra Captives. In addition, there were semisecret sales at ports before the Slaver's recorded detstination.

"Great improvements have been made to Liverpool, within these Twenty years [1769—89]. In the Construction of those Ships— The Space between the Decks is sufficiently large to contain [between 500 and 600] Negroes, and is plained very smooth and painted: — They are also provided with Wind Sails, and most of them have Ventilators."

—Testimony before Parliament by **Captain James Penny**: 1789

Typically, down in the hold the decks were layed out such that between one foot and three feet was allowed for height, no more than two feet for width, and less for front to back space. We had to lie down because there was only about 2 to 4 feet of space between our floor and the next level!

"EACH SLAVE HAD LESS ROOM THAN A MAN IN A COFFIN."

—Eric Williams: *Capitalism & Slavery*

"When I looked around the [slave] ship and saw a large furnace boiling and a multitude of black people chained together...I no longer doubted my fate... I fell motionless on the deck and fainted. [Later] I asked if we were not to be eaten by those white men with their horrible looks, red faces, and loose hair....

I received such a salutation in my nostrils...with the stench and crying together, I became so sick and low that I was not able to eat.... I now wished for the last friend, Death, to relieve me... I would have jumped over the side, but I could not... the crew used to watch us very closely... and I have seen some of these poor African prisoners, most severly cut for attempting to do so, and hourly whipped for not eating.... I had never seen among my people such instances of brutal cruelty, and this not only shown toward us blacks but also to some of the whites themselves. One white man in particular I saw...flogged so unmercifully.... that he died as a consequence of it; and they tossed him over the side as they would have done a brute.... The shrieks of the women and the groans of the dying rendered the whole scene of horror almost inconceivable..."

—Olaudah Equiano: 11 years old in 1756.

We had to either squat with knees and legs squeezed together and arms folded together or sit with another person wedged between our open legs for 8 to 14 hours every day for the weeks or months that it took to cross the Atlantic. The alternative was to lie flat on our backs for hours or days on wooden deck boards that were splintered and filthy with blood, human waste, parasitic bugs, flies, vomit.... We were shoulder to shoulder, chained to each other...and chained to the floor or the ship's hull.

MADNESS

"Madness, the distraction of despair, seems to possess them."

— Rev. Pascoe. G. Hill: *Fifty Days on Board a Slave-Vessel*

Some of our Ancetsors could not stand being in such confined quarters and went crazy— screaming, scratching, punching, kicking, throwing up. They were whipped, kicked and punched by the crew, their chains rubbing raw their skin, exposing blood and bone around ankles and wrists. They were embraced, soothed, held, or held down by their comrades. If that did not chill their delirium, they were taken up to the deck and whipped into silence or death.

Over the centuries, the thousands of days at sea, hundreds, thousands, of our Ancestors would jump overboard rather than continue to suffer in the Deathride of the MiddlePassage. The European slavers would try to stop this "escape" route by hanging heavy nets on the sides of the ships to catch leaping Africans. But many would find ways to get through the net. Some would start chewing the two inch thick hemp, thereby loosening the fibers enough to use their weight to rip the netting. Others would try to spread the net wide enough to get their head through... then force the rest of their body through and into the sharkfilled ocean. Still others would hide a splinter from a barrel or a piece of glass and would start cutting the netting before they were dragged up onto the deck.

"Slave cabin fever"—technically known as Claustrophobia— would happen more often when the slaveship was not filled to capacity and was cruising the African coastline or docked for weeks or months waiting for more Captives. By the 1600s, every slaveship Captain knew better than to allow his Captives on deck as long as Africa was in sight.

STIFLING AIR

The closeness of the place, and the heat of the climate, added to the number in the ship, which was so crowded that each had scarcely room to turn himself, almost suffocated us. This produced copious perspirations, so that the air soon became unfit for respiration, from a variety of loathsome smells, and brought on a sickness among the slaves, of which many died.

This wretched situation was again aggravated by the galling of the chains, now become insupportable, and the filth of the necessary tubs [slave toilets], into which the children often fell and were almost suffocated."

—Olaudah Equiano: The Interesting Narrative...of Olaudah Equiano

The portholes— if there were any—would be very small—about the size of a grapefruit. This would make it more difficult to jump out of the porthole... or to throw a baby overboard. There was so little ventilation that some prisoners would die from suffocation: they would be breathing less and less oxygen and more and more toxic fumes from the rotting bodies, human waste, and vomit..

Of course, the confinement, the mingling of arch enemies, the shortage of everything caused constant bickering, fighting, shoving, and stealing. This often resulted in weaker Captives being crushed to death or suffocating because they would be pushed to the bottom of the human pile gasping for air within the hole....

"Wednesday April 12, 1843. The night, however, being intensely hot and close, 400 wretched beings thus crammed into a hold 12 yards [36 feet] in length, 7 yards [21 feet] in breadth, and only 3 1/2 feet in height, speedily began to make an effort to reissue to the open air. Being thrust back, and striving the more to get out, the after-hatch was forced down on them.... They crowded to the grating, and clinging to it for air, completely barred its entrance. They strove to force their way through apertures, in length 14 inches and barley 6 inches in breadth, and, some instances, succeeded. The cries, the heat,— I may say, without exaggeration, 'the smoke of their torment,'—which ascended, can be compared to nothing earthly.

—Rev. Pascoe Grenfell Hill: *Fifty Days on Board a Slave-Vessel*

Around 1758, another British reverend, Stephen Hales, was "concerned" about the Human Cargo's ability to survive the "noxious putrid Air." Reverend Hales was not concerned about the enslavement of these humans, but about how to effectively bring these enslaved people to their Masters with minimum loss. He was not an abolitionist. He was about making slavery more efficient for capitalism's advancement! Thus, the good reverend developed "human powered ventilators to rid these areas of the bad air."

An 18th Century French slaveship Captain wrote to the good Reverend Hales that "in the year 1753, Ventilators were put into the Vessels in the Slave-trade... the happy Effect of which was, that instead of the loss of one-fourth of those valuable Cargoes in long passages from Africa to the French plantations, the loss seldom exceeded a twentieth."

JOIN US—

Experience Just a Taste of the Passage

By the time you arrive at the Deathship, you are not healthy. You have experienced the trauma of the capture; the miles and miles of the coffle's (the slave caravan) trek; the factories and dungeons.... Your diet has dissolved into nothing but a once a day gruel. You are filthy. Your hair has begun to mat, merging dirt and hair into a nest for bugs and bacteria. To make matters worse, you are dehydrating even before you are forced onto the slaveship.

You were given very little water in the dungeons—a pint or two a day was the average. During droughts and the dry season, even less.

NOW...

"...the slaves are affected with a very short ration of water."
—Dr. Luis Antônio de Oliveira Mendes: 1812

"We suffered very much for want of water but was denied all we needed. A pint a day was all that was allowed and many slaves died upon the passage."
—Testimony of Anonymous Captive African Man, Brazil 1854

"...the [African Captives are] labouring under the most famishing thirst... being in very few instances allowed more than a pint of water a day."
—Captain Hayes: 1844

"There is nothing which slaves during the middle passage suffer from so much as want of water."
—Thomas Buxton, 1844

"...in 1781, running short on water, the captain of the Zong ordered 132 Africans thrown overboard, because his insurance covered death by drowning but not from starvation"!
—Peter Kolchin: American Slavery

Below deck on the slaveship, the temperature was always hot (except for those few ships where Hales' Ventilators were used). 120 to 130 degrees day and night during the spring and summer months was typical. The humidity rarely dipped below 75%—usually, it was more like 90%. Lice, maggots and other parasites spread throughout the tightly packed human cargo. In fact, upon arrival at the slave selling port, every slave-ship was disinfected along with the Captives. You could not escape being a host for lice in your hair or maggots in your open sores.

Dehydration was a major cause of death on the slaveship. Remember, before you board you are already dying of thirst. And now that you are once again jammed into a dark hole at least 90° with high humidity, you are even more thirsty. But if you demand water, these ignorant white men just lash out at you with whips or clubs. So you try to learn how to conserve and rechannel your energy to minimize dehydration.

Note: African-American's Hypertension MiddlePassage Origins—

"...the nearly 400 year-long transatlantic slave trade may have acted as an evolutionary gate— individuals who survived passage through that gate would possess a different genetic makeup than those who did not. Virtually all subSaharan Africans transported to the Western Hemisphere between the 16th and 19th Centuries had to survive these conditions of excessive sodium loss; thus, all passed the same evolutionary gate. Today's descendants of the Captive Africans might possess a different genetic makeup than the descendants of Africans not trqansported across the Atlantic during the slave trade...

In today's high dietary sodium environment in the Western Hemisphere, these 'sodium-conserving' descen-dants of African slaves may be more susceptible to 'salt-sensitive' hypertension than the poulations descended from... Africans without this heritage."

Thomas Wilson & Clarence E. Grim, MD—
The Possible Relationship Between the Transatlantic Slave Trade and Hypertension in Blacks Today

For now, you are still at the pier, crouching or lying on your back, listening to the wails, whimpers, screams, groans, moans, prayers, curses, silences of your comrades in chains. You begin to sense the dizzying roll of the ship and begin to feel queasy... dizzy as they continue to load the ship. Someone very close to you is sick and throws up and then another two or three on the deck above you. You see the vomit above you and alongside you and you come close to passing out. You can barely breathe. You are trapped. You can't move a leg or arm without increasing someone else's misery. The chains rattle as we try to shift our bodies to get away from the running yellow brown stream and odor from next to us, from above us. The flies and mosquitoes begin to swarm around you. But you can't swipe at them without yanking your chained bretheren or sisteren.

Whips lash at us. Harsh guttural words spit from the mouths of white men. We don't understand their European words....but we Understand them. We begin to sense that the ship is in motion. Lots of noises on deck. You look into the eyes of the folk around you and you see the same madness you feel.

During the weeks since you were snatched from Home, you hear all the rumors, all the— what seemed to be— fantastic tales; all the premonitions about The Voyage of Death. You may not have believed all of the tales and rumors or you may have only believed that this was going to be a voyage to a new kind of Death-While-Living world. No one— except the most spiritually sensitive— could have forseen this present expierence:

The screams, moans, crying, coughing, wretching, wailing, prayercries are all around you ...in you ...You.

The pains, open sores, pus, mucous, blood, the foaming drool,

the chaincuts/gashes, bugs, rats... the hot smothering stinking air are all around you... in you ...You.

In fact, you have merged your Being with the total African Agony on board a vessel moving away from the Motherland.

Many hours later, when there is no sight of land to temp you to jump overboard and try to swim Home, you are allowed— still in chains— in small groups to come up to the deck for about 10 to 30 minutes— depending on the feelings of security by the crew... or how evil they or the Captain wants to be that day. When you are on

you check out the Enemy. Her eyes and her subtle smile tell you she's with you and was doing the same thing herself.

You look to the sky for birds, changes in the weather, for African Rescue Spirits. Instead, you see something that you had overlooked in assessing your Enemy: two whitemen perched way up on the masts looking

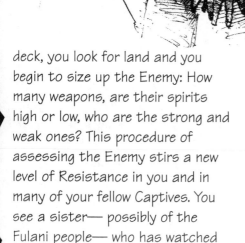

deck, you look for land and you begin to size up the Enemy: How many weapons, are their spirits high or low, who are the strong and weak ones? This procedure of assessing the Enemy stirs a new level of Resistance in you and in many of your fellow Captives. You see a sister— possibly of the Fulani people— who has watched

down on you with rifles at the ready. Suddenly, you feel the pain of not one whiplash but two, three.... The whites are growling something to you and pointing to the sky. You look up again and again you're lashed. This time the lashes are longer and fiercer cutting into you arms, legs and chest.

You get the message: Never look up at the men in the crow's nests!

Two of Them come at you with buckets of water....
You think these are kind ones until you scream
and shout from the buckets of salt walter burning into your open whip wounds. They throw you
back down into the hole laughing at you around
you through you. Your anger, your rage makes you
curse Them at the top of your voice in your native
tongue. They get the message and one of them
tosses another bucket of sea water down the
hole on you and a few of your chained comrades.
Some of them scream from the sting of the salt.

Suddenly, four of them enter your deck: two grab
you and two hold you down and rechain you to
the others and the ship's floor. They spit on you
and kick you. They leave as suddenly and thunderously as they came.

You are lucky this time: there was no rape: no
grabbing of your breasts or twisting your vagina...or axe handles up it....

Your Fulani comrade stumbles down into the hold
and is rechained. When the laughing and grunting
whitemen go, she turns to you and passes you
the herb-bag that's strung around her neck by a
leather strap. Unable to understand each other's
language, she uses hand signs on how to apply
the herbs to your wounds.

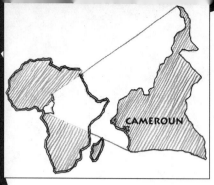

CAMEROUN

Eventually, among the 185 African women and 40 girls (12 years old and under) aboard someone is able to translate between the **Fulani** sister and yourself: a young woman of stature from a small village among the **Seke** People (in today's Cameroun). You talk in low whispers and moans both to confuse the crew and because you are in pain and weak with hunger, dizziness, and dehydration. It's been more than 12 hours since you had water or food. You ate last on land. It was the usual slop: yams, dried plaintains and stale corn mush. You still can't get use to eating with dirty hands out of dirty wooden bowls food that frequently would have worms or mealy bugs sprinkled throughout. Not even the animals in your village ate this badly!

"The diet ... while on board, consists chiefly of horse-beans boiled to the consistency of a pulp [i.e. gooey], yams and rice and sometimes of a small quantitiy [a few ounces per Captive] of beef or pork. The latter are frequently taken from the provisions laid in for the sailors. They sometimes make use of a sauce composed of palm-oil mixed with flour, water and pepper, which the sailors call slabber-sauce. Yams are the favorite food of the Eboe or Bight negroes and rice or corn of those from the Gold & Windward Coasts...."
—Dr. Alexander Falconbridge, slaveship surgeon: 1788

Suddenly, thunderously, the whitemen — 6 at a time —descend into your hovel with large wooden bowls of crudely crushed yams and some brownish thing you've never seen before. Food... of sorts.

"They are fed twice a day [lie], at 10 in the morning, and 4 in the evening, which is the time they are aptest to mutiny, being all upon deck [lie]; therefore all that time, what of our men are not employ'd in distributing their victuals [food] to them, and settling them, stand to their arms..."
—English Slaveship Captain: 1693

The 'food' stinks stronger than all the foul odors around you. You take a sample to your lips on your finger tip and spit it out in revulsion. The others react similarly. Except there are a few who are eating as if it was a homecooked meal! Your Fulani comrade and the translating sister turn to you and nod solidarity. Because of how you handled yourself up on deck and your defiance during the weeks in the slave dungeons you have gained respect among the strong women. Soon other sisters join in the nod of solidairty. You start to rhythmically pound the deckfloor and others follow.

"For your own safety as well as mine, You'll have the needfull Guard over your Slaves, and put not too much confidence in the Women nor Children lest they happen to be Instrumental to your being surprised which might be fatall."

—**Samuel Waldo,** Owner of Slaveship **Africa** to his captain: 1734

"Numberless quarrels take place among them during their meal; more especially when they are put upon short allowance, which frequently happens..."

—**Alexander Falconbridge,** Slaveship surgeon: 1788

107

A cleaner looking whiteman comes down into the hold with a curious half-frightened, half-amused look on his face. He grunts something that seems like a question. One of the sisters trying to sit up under a 2-foot ceiling is speaking in his language: "We want food! Not garbage! Or we all die!" You don't understand a word, but you understand her force and self-confidence. As soon as she finishes talking in his language, she starts the rhythmic pounding again.... And everybody joins in— including the 220 African men and 85 boys on board. Now the whole ship has become a Drum of Defiance, a Demanding Drum. No words are chanted. Just the pounding that goes on for about an hour before the same whiteman returns to the hole and shouts with a wild eye smile: "All right! All right! Stop the drumming! Your better food is coming!" The Sister Translator speaks Twi and that gets quickly translated creating the African woman wail (ululations) of thanks to spread throughout the decks. But what you received as "better" food turns out to be almost as bad as the first slop. This time, there is little more seasoning and a slightly fresher taste to the gruel.... Still no water. You have a choice of urinating or defecating where you lay or try to squat or use....

...the three or four large buckets, of a conical form, being near two feet in diameter at the bottom, and only one foot at the top, and indepth about twenty-eight inches; in which, when necessary, the negroes have recourse... [Often when our Captive Ancestors try to reach these 'toilets' they would] tumble over their companions, in consequence of their being shackled...

[Some] desist from the attempt, and as the necessities of nature are not to be repelled, ease themselves as they lie..."

—Alexander **Falconbridge**, Slaveship Surgeon: 1789

For all the African Captives, this proves to be the most humiliating and dehumanizing thing of all. Tears of shame and anger flow. You curse the whiteman, the blackman who traded you for a barrel of rum and some little knives and the African Gods whom you feel have allowed this to happen to you and millions of others.

> "Friday, May 12, 1843— I have to-day witnessed a spectacle such as I had frequently heard to have occurred in slave-vessels, but hardly know how to describe. In a tub, placed on the slave-deck, for necessary purposes, a boy was found, who had fallen backward, and too weak to extricate himself, was smothered in it. He appeared quite dead; but, on some water being thrown over him, showed some symptoms of returning life, though only for a few hours."
>
> —Rev. Pascoe G. Hill: Fifty Days on Board a Slave-Vessel

Miserable moaning screaming hours pass as you drift into an angry sleep (in fact, you will sleep no more than 2 or 3 hours a night for the entire voyage... leaving you mentally and physically drained with red eyes and aches in every joint.). Then thunder and drunken laughter cuts through the hole. Three whitemen with a lamp stumble down and start searching and asking: "Which of you nigga wenches speaks English?" Sister Translator speaks up and they grab her and unshackle her and push her up on deck.

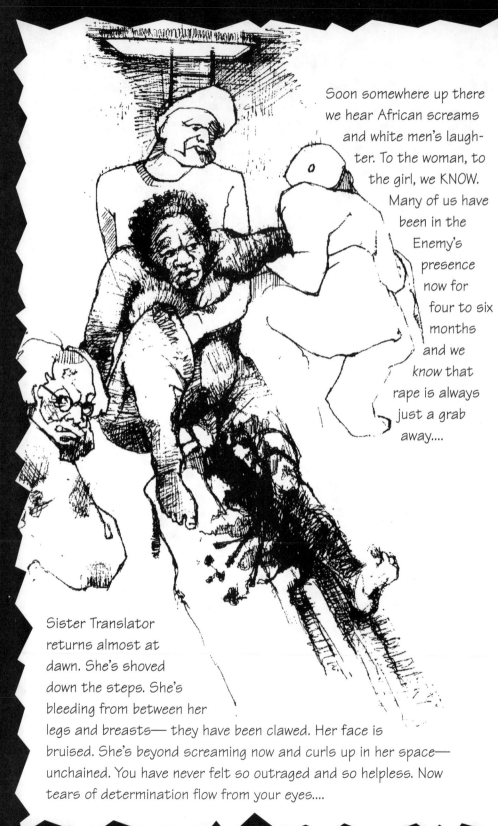

Soon somewhere up there we hear African screams and white men's laughter. To the woman, to the girl, we KNOW. Many of us have been in the Enemy's presence now for four to six months and we know that rape is always just a grab away....

Sister Translator returns almost at dawn. She's shoved down the steps. She's bleeding from between her legs and breasts— they have been clawed. Her face is bruised. She's beyond screaming now and curls up in her space— unchained. You have never felt so outraged and so helpless. Now tears of determination flow from your eyes....

The Ships' Surgeon: A Veterinarian at Best

Just as you sense dawn, this same cleaner looking white man from the day before comes down into the hole and searches out Sister Translator. He looks over her wounds like you would look at a hurt sheep. He mumbles something to her and returns to the upper deck. Sister Translator tells us he is the whiteman's "medicine man" called "surgeon." You try that word out: "Surgeon." It doesn't feel right in your mouth. It doesn't sound right or good. You decide not to trust this surgeon...

Africans had very good reasons not to trust the ship's surgeon. He was usually a very poorly educated mockery of a Western doctor, or an alcholic doctor no long trusted to treat whitefolks, or some doctor banished to a slaveship because of a bad medical judgement, or a veterinarian who liked to travel the seas... In short, they were not good doctors, nor did they think to treat enslaved Africans as part of Humanity. They had no idea about the African traditional ways of staying healthy and strong because they assumed Africans had no medical knowledge. [When, in fact, it was Africans— through the Ancient Egyptians and Moors— that gave Europe its medical foundation!]

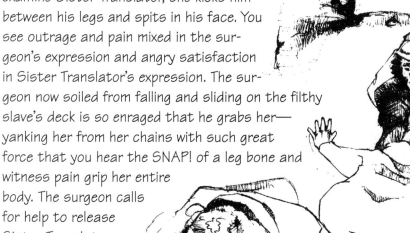

As the surgeon bends over to further examine Sister Translator, she kicks him between his legs and spits in his face. You see outrage and pain mixed in the surgeon's expression and angry satisfaction in Sister Translator's expression. The surgeon now soiled from falling and sliding on the filthy slave's deck is so enraged that he grabs her— yanking her from her chains with such great force that you hear the SNAP! of a leg bone and witness pain grip her entire body. The surgeon calls for help to release Sister Translator.

Once she is released, they drag her upstairs onto the deck with her left leg dangling with exposed bone, muscle, and blood. You hear lots of scuffling and whiplashes— but no screams or moans or whimpers or curses from Sister Translator.

You see the early morning sunlight slicing through the cracks and the portholes above you. You and other women worry about the silence on deck. Moments pass like days... you want to know if Sister Translator is alright.

Suddenly and thunderously many crew members come crashing down into the hole and unchain all of the African women and girls and force you hurriedly up on deck. You wonder why. Why are they taking all of us up? Have we reached their homeland already? Are they going to let us go back home?

NO.

When you finally adjust your eyes to the morning brightness, you see some of your sister Captives with a most frightening look of shock on their faces. You turn in the direction they are facing and see what has zombified them.

There was Sister Translator alright. Dead... But more than dead.

She was hanging and swinging by her tongue from the main mast. Naked. There was a giant hook through her tongue and the roof of her mouth. Her eyes bulged in disbelief.

DEAD.. BUT MORE THAN DEAD.

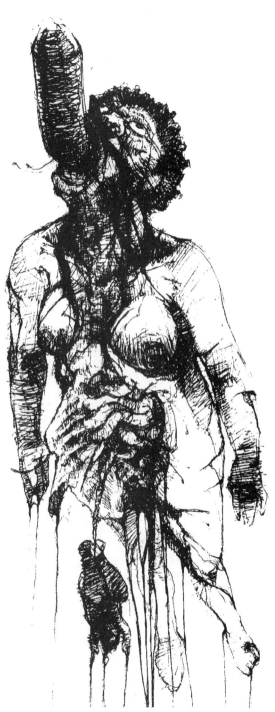

As you look down from her once beautiful, now monstrous face, you see her stomach was crudely ripped opened to show not only her bowels and intestines but also to show an African fetus dangling on her umbilical chord.

You want to turn away and throw up but you can't. Something is forcing you to take in every detail, every swing of her body, every sound, every silence. There are many other Sisters — girls and women— who are just as transfixed.

Who are REMEMBERING. Who are

NEVER FORGETTING.

Now that this Surgeonman sees that he has the attention of every-body, he silently and with great drama walks over to Sister Translator and swiftly cuts the umbilical chord and catches the baby/fetus and all in one motion flings it high over the deck.

You watch the African child-to-be. It looks like it was flying. Flying Home. You can only imagine it clearing the slave-nets and splashing into the ocean... being gobbled up by the trailing sharks.

The surgeon is grinning with his feet spread wide and his bloody hands on his hips and growls something with his red eyes directly at YOU!

White laughter fills your head. The crews' boots shuffle all around you; pushing you back down into the black hole.

Can things get worse? Are these humans or beasts from another world? Do I die now? Or wait for the right time to take some of them with me down Death's road? Do I fight to stay alive to put these monsters out of power? Do I try to be like them? Learn their ways? Do I submit to their ways?

These are questions drumming in your head like many different rhythms beating at the same time. You look around at your sisters and see that many now are giving in to the Enemy. They have vacant eyes, sloped shoulders and a frightened or bewildered look.

You whisper to your chain mates: "We can't let them kill us! We can't let them treat us worse than rats! Our sister did not die for that!" Your words spread through all the languages. Many sisters— old and young— signal solidarity with their glittering eyes... But, by now, there are many sisters who have already decided to submit to the ways of whitefolk.

Later, the African men are subjected to the sight of Sister Translator. You could not see them. You could only hear some of the commotion. There are shouts of fear and anger. You think you hear scuffling and punching and white screams. A Splash! Two Splashes! More...! Gunfire! SILENCE.

"I ordered the Linguist to acquaint the men-Negroes, 'That now they might judge, no one that killed a white Man should be spared.'"

—**William Snelgrave**, Slaveship Captain: 1727

"Captain Harding... [made] them first eat the Heart and Liver of one of [the whites who was] killed.."

"The woman he [Captain Harding] hoisted up by the Thumbs, whipp'd and slashed her with Knives, before the other Slaves till she died."

—The Surgeon of the English Slaveship **Robert:** 1721

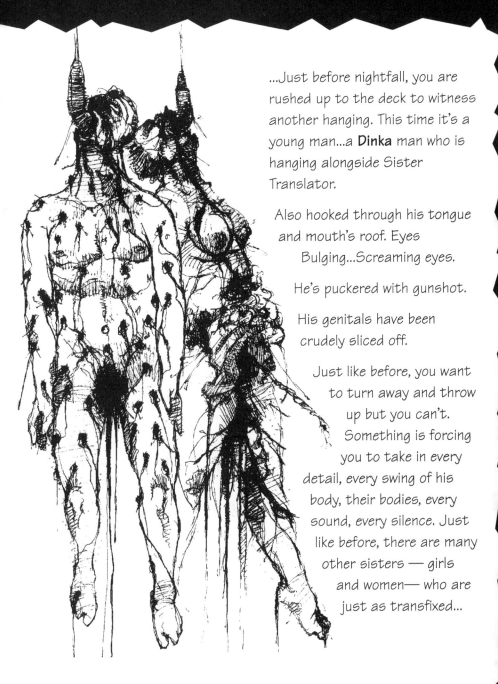

...Just before nightfall, you are rushed up to the deck to witness another hanging. This time it's a young man...a **Dinka** man who is hanging alongside Sister Translator.

Also hooked through his tongue and mouth's roof. Eyes Bulging...Screaming eyes.

He's puckered with gunshot.

His genitals have been crudely sliced off.

Just like before, you want to turn away and throw up but you can't. Something is forcing you to take in every detail, every swing of his body, their bodies, every sound, every silence. Just like before, there are many other sisters — girls and women— who are just as transfixed...

Who are REMEMBERING.

Who are

NEVER FORGETTING...

...Many days pass. Weeks. You fall into a miserable almost sleepless routine: sometimes soothing women who are on the edge of sanity; sometimes joining in the songwails calling for dreaming about Home; helping the young girls overcome their shock of loss of innocence and fun... their witness to monstrous violence and whitemen's sadistic pleasures. But you have never given up Hope for Victory over these Invaders and Robbers.

You (and you *Know*, *Feel* other sisters and brothers are thinking the same way) are always scheming about **Freedom**....

"We had the misfortune to lose 36 of the best slaves we had by an Insurrection; this unlucky affair happened...when there was only the Boatswaine, Carpenter, 3 White people and myself [the slave-ship's surgeon]... We had 160 slaves on board and were that day let out of the Deck Chains in order to was, about 2 O'Clock... They began by seizing upon the Boatswain... but he soon got dis-engaged... after receivinga wound on his breast and one under his Chin... they continued to [throw] Staves, bil-lets of wood, etc., and in endeavoring to get down the Baricado, or over it for upwards of 40 minutes, when finding they could not effect it all the Fantee and most of the Accra Men Slaves jumped over board."
—Surgeon on Rhode Island-based slaveship **Hope**: 1776

Over the months together in stressful bondage, your body's biological rhythms has synchronized with most of the other Captive Sisters. You remember that this also happened to you when you spent 7 months living with other young women of your large village preparing for womanhood. Most of the 65 initiates had their "period" together.

But you also notice that some of your Captive Sisters have had no menstruation. And they are not pregnant. You think: This Deathvoyage is turning us into very different Beings. Our bodies and their functions are not ours to control. We will all never be the same: some will be stronger; some will crack and die, others will commit suicide... and still others will collapse into a trance and become the Whiteman's Zombie.

...One day as you finally start to menstruate (have your period), many of the other women and some of the girls also start! None of you have your traditional methods of handling this natural process, so the constantly bloodied and filthy deck is beginning to be covered with even more blood.

"By letters from Capt. Hopkins in a brig belonging to Providence, arrived here [Newport] from Antigua from the coast of Africa, we learn that soon after he left the [African] coast, the number of his men being reduced by sickness, he was obliged to permit some of the slaves to come upon deck to assist the people [crew members]. These slaves contrived to release others, and the whole rose upon the people, and endeavoured to get possession of the vessel; but was happily prevented by the captain and his men, who killed, wounded and forced overboard 80 of them, which obliged the rest to submit."

—**Newport Mercury** newspaper: 18 Nov. 1765

Why?

During the 5 centuries of the TransAtlantic Slave Trade the population and migratory practices of Atlantic sharks changed dramtically. There were dispro-portionately more sharks and they fol-lowed the hundreds of Slaveships criss-crossing the Atlantic and the Caribbean. This has resulted in today's Atlantic shark being quantitavely and qualitatively different than the Pacific shark: they have acquired more of a "taste" for human flesh than their Pacific kin!

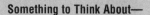

But you and your Fulani Sister, your Mandingo Sister, your Fon Sister, your Ibo Sister, your Yoruba Sister... many of your sisters trying to survive and make sense of this terror vow **to fight to keep control over your Flesh and Souls. No matter what the White Monster tries to turn you into.**

The young girls, many 7 to 12 years old, are now little women: never to play the children's games again. You have seen them whipped and abused just like grown women. Some have died of diseases or the whippings or the gang rapes you could only witness through the screams, grunts and white laughter filtering through the hole almost every day or night on the now weeks at sea. You and a few of your Sisters have quietly given memorial ceremonies for these little lost souls that have been killed and tossed to the sharks following the Slaveship.

After the first 30 days at sea, you are beyond tears and are filled with rage. You learn how to stop the rage from eating you alive. You stare the whiteman down and no longer cry out when whipped or punched.

The morning they first came for you, they had to drag you limp like a sack to the bed of the Captain's main helper they called "First Mate." This was the same whiteman who raped four young girls, forcing one—just 12 years old—to commit suicide. This was the same whiteman who mutilated the body of a Ibo woman after she fought back.

But first two men threw buckets of salt water on you and scrubbed you with crude soap and oiled you down with palm oil while two other men with guns leered into every pore of your body. They cuffed you with iron and wooden cuffs so that your hands hung helplessly in front of you. You felt humiliation and rage together so intense you could taste it.

A few of your Brothers were on deck working on something and saw you being prepared for the First Mate's bed. You saw helpless rage and embarrassment in their eyes— except for one. You could sense his cunning ways... probably a seasoned warrior. The scars from whiplashes across his chest and back told you all. Will you see him again? Will he make it alive to the whiteman's land? Will he run away? Or stay and organize?

Suddenly you are flat on your back and your cuffed hands are loosely tied onto one of the bedposts. Your eyes blur. You fight to keep your legs closed. But the First Mate is too strong for your weakened body's resistance. You scream and he laughs standing naked with wild hungry eyes. You realize that he gets even more worked up from your screams. He whips you with his belt while shouting (curses?) things that help turn his red eyes redder. You let your mind take you away from what was happening to your flesh: the scraping, pawing, groping, grunting, growling and drooling like a bull in heat. The First Mate became some annoying painful animal inside of you... around you. You are lucky this morning. You sensed he would be finished with you momentarily. Meanwhile... *your Soul went Home to remember sweet laughing things from the past.* It was over in less than fifteen minutes but it felt like hours.

The First Mate rolls off of you and begins to snore.

NOW'S YOUR CHANCE!

Chance to do what? There's a guard outside the door. You see the knife and think that he would know it's missing. Kill him? No. You want to live. Instead, you feel that you can untie your cuffed hands and do so. You take a strand of his hair and you spit on his hairy red chest and walk softly to the door.... The guard pushes you back down steps to the main deck and into your hold.

You feel dirtier than ever. Just before the guard pushes your head down to the slave decks below you see the scarred warrior again and he shouts in your language: "Hold fast, Sister! We've got a plan!" A whiplash strikes his shoulder. His eyes lock on you as the lash draws blood. He, too, is beyond pain. In that instant, you know that the Scarred Warrior will survive and struggle.

And you have a plan, too! For the First Mate. All the Sisters knew what happened to you and most show sympathetic eyes. The guard takes off your cuffs and reattaches your chains to the deck and the other women. You pass the whiteman's strand of hair to one of the spiritual leaders and she starts to perform some ritual you are not familar with since you are Seke and she is Yoruba. But you sense its power. She says: "The First Mate will fall ill, very ill, before we see land. And he will never rape again. Yememya & Oshun will see to that!"

More days on the endless water. The food begins to be served in smaller and smaller portions and looks and taste worse. You learn how to sip the gruel between your clenched teeth so that you don't swallow maggots, other larvae and other unknown things. You may get a cup of water a day, but the water is dirtier... with all kinds of things dead and alive floating around in it.

Two storms that brought the sea into the ship and shouts and screams from the whitemen on deck have left you believing the world is finally ending. You believe that some of them died from the storms tossing them overboard... or by sickness. You also believe that some of the African men have died during the storms. You heard their chains dragging across the deck during the storms. You heard desperate whiplashes strike flesh.

"Some wet and blowing weather having occasioned the port-holes to be shut and the grating [to the ship's deck] to be covered, fluxes and fevers among the negroes ensued. While they were in this situation, I frequently went down among them till at length their rooms[!?] became so extremely hot as to be only bearable for a short time... The floor of their rooms was so covered with the blood and mucus which had proceeded from them in consequence of the flux, that it resembled a slaughterhouse... Numbers of slaves having fainted they were carried upon deck where several of them died and the rest with great difficulty were restored....."

—Dr. Alexander Falconbridge—
Slaveship Surgeon: 1788

You and your Sisters were flooded for two days after each storm. There was about a foot of water on your dark deck. This meant that you could not lie down. And there was not enough space for you to sit up unless all of you folded into the fetal position and leaned on each others back so that your face would be out of the filthy water. During and after each of the storms, the heat and humidity would intensify and many would get very sick and die.

You would be allowed on deck for an hour while the crew and two or three African men would go down in the hole to retrieve the dead and try to bail out some of the filthy water. It is then that you notice that there are less crew members... and those that have survived look very weak. You search for the First Mate, hoping that the last storm got him. But he's still there: looking healthier and more evil than ever.

You think: "Yemenya and Oshun are not powerful enough for these whitemen!"

PIRATES!

On the 65th day (you know this because to help maintain your sanity, you have been tallying the days by scratching a mark on the hull with your chain every morning) just before dawn, you hear whitemen shouting like you never heard before. There was a lot of fear in their voices.

Then came the gunfire. Thunderous but distant— like you never heard before. Then a loud explosive splash! A few of the Sisters are able to see out of the tiny portholes another ship pulling up along side the Slaveship. The Commotion up on deck intensifies. There is an explosion up on deck and loud gunfire. Screams of pain and sounds of bodies falling hard onto the deck.

You are frightened beyond what you have already been. The Sisters who can see the other ship say that it is damaged with a hole in its side and leaning into the water. More thunderous booms from up on deck. You can hear the crack of the other ship's mast and muffled screams of wounded and dying men. Yells and hoots of victory resound up on deck. You learn from the other Sisters that the other sinking ship's crew was left to the sharks.

By mid-afternoon you are allowed up on deck. Six whitemen's bodies lay wrapped in old sail cloth with their caps or hats placed on their chests. Some sort of whiteman's ceremony is in progress. The Captain— sad-faced— holds a black book and a gold cross. The crew's heads are bowed and solemn. You look around and notice three things: for the first time all surviving Captives— men, women and children are up on deck; one of the hats of the dead belong to the First Mate; there are more and different birds circling about. The Yoruba Sister smiles. And for the first time in weeks, months you too smile. *Yemenya and Oshun did avenge the Sisters of this Deathship.*

Now, after some 80 days on the Slaveship, there are days and nights of relative calm. The surviving crew and captain allow you a little more time on deck and a little more food (only because there are less crew to eat!). Even a little dried meat and saltfish is thrown into the gruel. You are even given limes or lemons to suck on (to help fight scurvy). The sisters hold onto the limes and lemons to later rub them on their bodies to help heal the scratches, sores and infections. Because of more food, there is less squabbling, pushing and shoving during meals. The men are even treated to a little tobacco and rum... and you and the other women were given shiny, gaudy and cheap beads of many colors. The captain thinks this will make you forget your chains and enslaved conditions.

"...the utmost Attention is paid to the keeping up their Spirits and to endulge them in all their little Humours."

—**Captain James Penny** (of Liverpool): 1789

Now there is a calm... a false calm. You know it is a false and temporary calm because you are still chained, guns are still pointed at you, whips fly, your sick comrades never get treated, and whitemen shout and scream at you... and continue to rape your sisters and young boys.

This false calm is over quickly. Many of your Brothers start gambling— not for money— but for tobacco or leftover rum. And this now daily gambling leads to arguments and fights. You are still unable to see them when they are on deck and you are separated below deck. But you can hear the shouting and scuffling, chains dragging and bodies falling. You also hear the whiteman's whips and shouts for calm.

Among the Sisters there are now more bickering and fights about the cheap beads, extra food scraps, space,the extra strips of cloth thrown down the hold by the crew. Everyone's nerves are on end and tension is the order of the day or night.

You realize that it will be harder now to unite for the Freedomfight. The Captives are divided now not just along different cultural/language backgrounds but also greed over cheap trinkets thrown to Us by the white Master.

You still can't sleep: the moans, groans, coughing, wheezing, screams, curses in various languages, lying in filth, the stench of Death and Misery, the chains and shackles rubbing your arms and legs raw. You feel yourself drifting into madness, delirium. But you are determined not to give in to this white Hell.

So you struggle to focus on a scheme to be Free. Escape. Kill your captors and go Home. You feel the need to talk about your Plan to the Sisters you *think* you can trust.

TRANSFORMATION:

Body & Soul

Your stay on the deathship lasts 88 days before you see land again. You are exhausted, drained... as if you have been running for months. You have aged in body beyond your nineteen years. You have lost about a third of your weight and some of your hair. You can feel the redness in your eyes. Your eyesight has deteriorated. You only have half of your teeth left. Your once beautiful blemish-free chocolate brown silky smooth skin is now covered with sores, pock-marks, scars and has turned a gray-yellowbrown. Your clothes are stinking rags barely covering you below your waist.

Only those 7 or 8 Sisters who have let the crew know that they don't mind being their whores and survived their violence look a little healthier than you do.

"When the ship makes the land, and have their port in view... then, and not before, they venture to release the men slaves from their irons, and then, the sight of the land, and the freedom from long and painful confinement, usually excite in them a degree of alacrity, and a transient feeling of joy.

The prisoner leaps to lose its chains. But this joy is short-lived indeed. The condition of the unhappy slave is a continual process from bad to worse."

—Captain John Newton: 1788

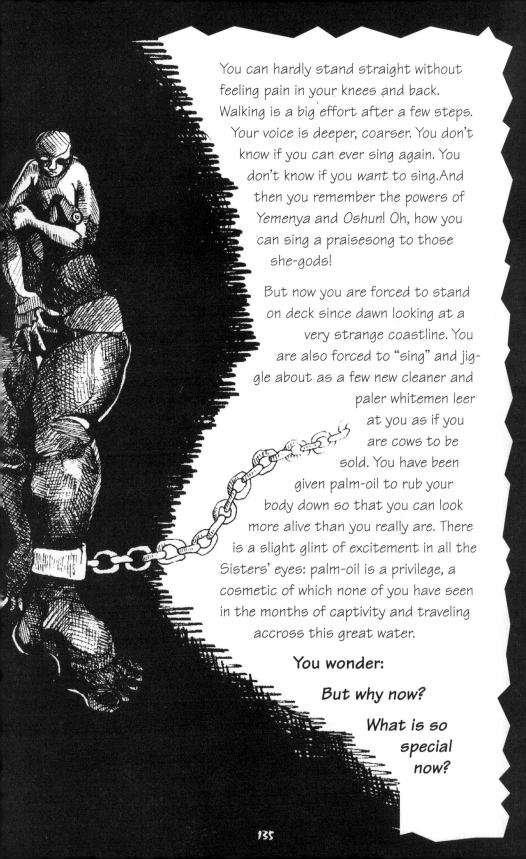

You can hardly stand straight without feeling pain in your knees and back. Walking is a big effort after a few steps. Your voice is deeper, coarser. You don't know if you can ever sing again. You don't know if you *want* to sing. And then you remember the powers of *Yemenya* and *Oshun*! Oh, how you can sing a praisesong to those she-gods!

But now you are forced to stand on deck since dawn looking at a very strange coastline. You are also forced to "sing" and jiggle about as a few new cleaner and paler whitemen leer at you as if you are cows to be sold. You have been given palm-oil to rub your body down so that you can look more alive than you really are. There is a slight glint of excitement in all the Sisters' eyes: palm-oil is a privilege, a cosmetic of which none of you have seen in the months of captivity and traveling accross this great water.

You wonder:

But why now?

**What is so
special
now?**

Captain John Newton's Logbook from May 23, 1751 to July 2, 1751

Thursday 23rd May... Buryed a man slave (no.34)

Wednesday 28th May... Buryed a boy slave (no. 86) of a flux

Wednesday 12th June... Buryed a man slave (no. 84) of a flux, which he had been struggling with near 7 weeks...

Thursday 13th of June . . . This morning buryed a woman slave (no. 47). Know not what to say she died of for she has not been properly alive since she first came on board.

Thursady 20th June. . . buryed a man (no.140) of a flux, and a boy (no. 170) of the gravel and stoppage of urine...

Monday 24 June. . . buryed a slave boy (no.158) and a girl (no. 172)

Tuesday 2 July. . . buryed a man (no. 2) of a flux which he has sustained about three months. A man (no.36) died of a flux...

On Wednesday July 3, 1751 Captain Newton's slaveship, *Duke of Argyle*, was piloted into the Antiguan harbour of St. John's. (Our Ancestors, who, in their transition from being African to being negro subhumans, were referred to only by number, were buried unceremoneously: tossed overboard to the waiting sharks like dead cattle.

The Scramble Ordeal

"The survivors of this gruelling ordeal were sold either on the ships or in slave markets in American ports. In New England, where there was a large 'retail' demand [before the North abolished slavery in its territory] slaves were sold in taverns, stores and warehouses. They were also 'shown,' as the ads put [it], in the homes of merchants."

—Lerone Bennett, Jr.: *Before the Mayflower*

You look closer at your brothers on deck and they too are palm-oiled down. Some are still able to stand in proud defiance staring the whitemen in the eye. Others have become seasoned or are too weak and sick and in great pain and are bent over... looking at the deck with shoulders bent and Death in their eyes, shuffling and dragging their chains as they are whipped into a "dance" to show how sprightly they are.

"The poor astonished negroes were so much terrified by these proceedings, that several of them, through fear [jumped overboard], climbed over the walls of the courtyard, and ran wild about the town; but were soon hunted down and retaken.... The women in particular clung to each other in agonies scarcely to be conceived, shrieking through excess of terror, at the savage manner in which their brutal purchasers rushed upon, and seized them."

—Alexander Falconbridge,
Slaveship Surgeon: 1789

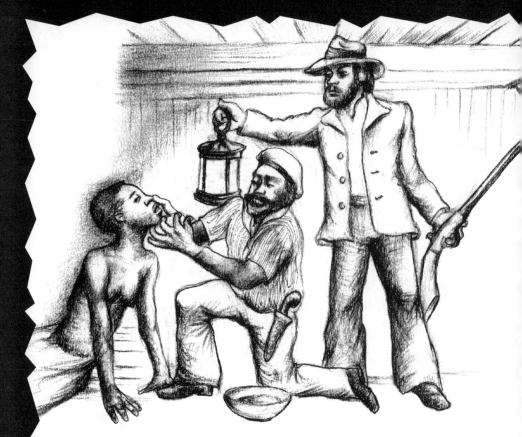

You feel for them in their despair. The MiddlePassage has "seasoned" them. They are accepting their fate as defined by the white man. You recommit yourself: never accept that way of living; of submitting to the white man; of joining the Living Dead: the Zombies.

(These "new" whitemen were called Scramblers because they would rush on board a Slaveship before it docks and brave the filfth and stench so as to get the best price on the healthiest looking Captives. They would separate their pick out from the rest and have them placed in a corner of the deck. Hence, the origin of the capitalist term "To corner the Market.")

"[Planters] buy them out of the Ship, where they find them stark naked, and therefore cannot be deceived in any outward infirmity. They choose them as they do Horses in a Market; the strongest, youthfullest, and most beautiful, yield the greatest price."

—**Richard Ligon**, *A True and Exact History of the Island of Barbados*

The new whitemen start pointing to and poking at various Captives and you watch as they are unchained and rechained in corners of the deck... 60 men and teenage boys in all. You have no idea what these strange rituals mean.

Rumorword spreads that they are the first to be killed on the new land... some sort of whiteman's sacrifice.

No. They are the ones selected to return Home!

No. They are food for these new grunting faces.

No. They are to be bought by these men... to be their slaves for life... and the life of their children... and their children's children....

The last rumor seems to you the most outrageous because it is a curse that lasts for generations. It is a horror that you pass on to your children. For you, a *Seke*, that is unbelieveable... something so unhuman that it is beyond your comprehension.

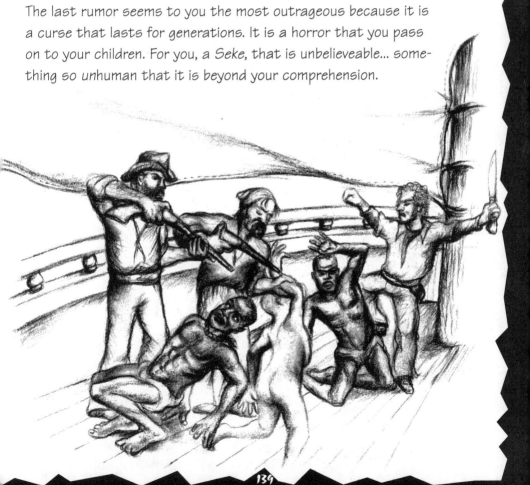

As the whitemen go about their noisy and boisterous rituals, you and the others take in the strange land. Buildings like you've never seen before... all pressed together along narrow streets with boards hanging with all kinds of strange markings. You see many Africans running, carrying heavy loads, pushing or pulling wheeled vehicles. You also see huge four legged animals allowing men to sit on their backs!

Whitemen with too many clothes on for the heat of the morning....

....and white women. For the first time you see their females! They too were pale and very overdressed with cloth up to their necks and scraping the ground. Some carried a frilly cloth on a stick to cover themselves from the sun. Others had little African boys running with them or sitting with them in their carriages fanning them.

You looked for your Sisters on land. You have to search further inland to see a few Black faces sweeping, washing, scrubbing, carrying heavy loads on their heads.

No African seems to be walking. They all seem to be running or straining themselves with heavy burdens.

You now have a sense of what lies ahead for you in this strange land run by whitemen: you are to be a beast; a vessel both for the whims of the white master and for bringing forth more African laborers from your womb.

For the first time tears start to trickle down your cheeks as you think of what you and your comrades have gone through to reach these shores and only to have to face even more horror. But these are not tears of sorrow and depression.

These are tears of rage...
Fierce Black Rage....

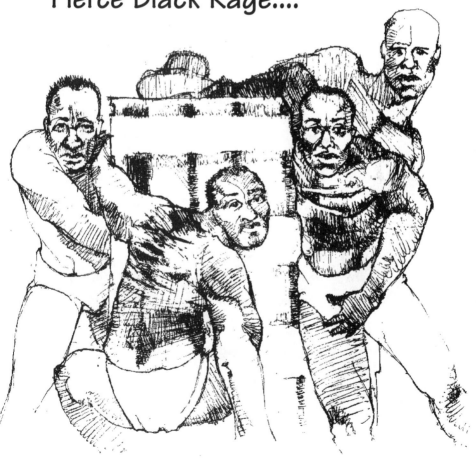

Your angry contemplations are cut short because you sense someone staring at you. You turn and see this whiteman from the New Land looking at you in the same way as the First-Mate did: with grimy lust. He says something to the Captain and the captain laughs and nods while gesturing at you to come to him. This whiteman has a partner who comes down onto the deck and proceeds to turn you around, poke and grab every conceiveable part of your body: mouth, lips, teeth, toungue, breasts, hips, arms, armpits, ears, vagina, anus, feet, nose, eyes, hair, thighs, knees... He turns to the whiteman (who has never let his eyes drift from you) and gives him an approving smile and gesture.

Before you can realize what is happening you are pushed away from your Sister shipmates and into a small crowd of African men from many parts of West Africa... but no Seke. You turn to try to catch the eye of your Yoruba Sister, but she and the other women are being shoved back down below deck and you are being pushed up onto a rope ladder on the side of the ship. You call out her name: Abiola!. Abiola! Shipmate Abiola! But all you get is a bruising shove and a slap across the face from the probing whiteman.

"Various shreds of evidence suggest that some of the earliest social bonds to develop in the coffles, in the factories and, especially, during the MiddlePassage were of a dyadic (two person) nature. Partly, perhaps, because of the genreal policy of keeping men and women separate, they were usually between members of the same sex. The bond between shipmates, those who shared passage on the same slaver, is the most striking example. In widely scattered parts of Afro-America, the 'shipmate' relationship became a major principle of social organization and continued for decades or even centuries to shape ongoing social relations.

In Jamaica, for example, we know that the term 'shipmate' was synonymous ... with brother or sister...."

—S.W. Mintz & Richard Price:*The Birth of African American Culture*

"...the dearest word [shipmate] and bond of affectionate sympathy amongst the Africans... so strong were the bonds between shipmates that sexual intercourse between them... was considered incestuous... [and] looked upon each other's children mutually as their own. It was customary for children to call their parents' shipmates' uncle and aunt."

—J. Kelly, British traveler to Jamaica, 1838

"Sippi" means "shipmate" among the early enslaved Africans in Suriname, eventually transforming to mean "plantation Mate" as the centuries of enslavement wore on. Today, among the Saramaka people (the Maroons— or runaways— of Suriname) "sibi" means a special relationship between two people who have simultaneously suffered something very traumatic. "Sibi" is how they would address each other.

Other variations on "shipmate":

Máti— Suriname

Malungo— Brazil

Malongue— Trinidad

Batiment— Haiti

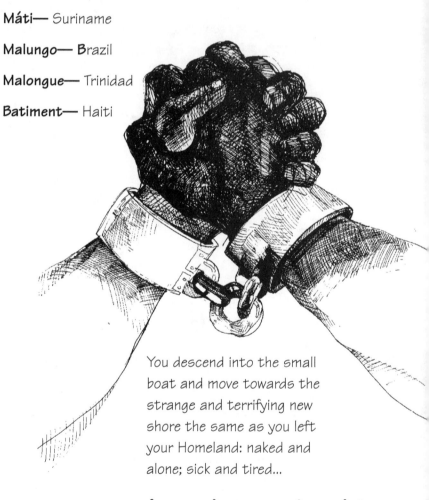

You descend into the small boat and move towards the strange and terrifying new shore the same as you left your Homeland: naked and alone; sick and tired...

but determined to be FREE!

ON THE NEW SOIL:

Planting the Resistance Seed

"We were not many days in the merchant's custody [in Barbados of 1756] before we were sold after the usual manner, which is this: On a signal given (at the beat of a drum) the buyers rush at once into the yard where the slaves are confined, and make choice of that parcel they like best. The noise and clamoor with which this is attended and the eargerness visible in the countenances of the buyers serve not a little to increase the apprehensions of the terrified Africans, who may well be supposed to consider them as the ministers of that destruction to which they think themselves devoted. In that manner, without scruple, are relations and friends separated, most of them never to see each other again. I remember in the vessel in which I was brought over, in the men's apartment there were several brothers who, in the sale, were sold in different lots; and it was very moving on this occasion to see and hear their cries at parting...."

—Oludiah Equiano

New Dungeons and Barracoons—

Friday June 2 and Monday June 19, 1843—"I was not prepared for the feeling generally evinced by the negroes on coming into port, which is that of evident anxiety and apprehension. Whether it arise from their thinking less even of present ills than of 'others which they not of,' or from some particular foreboding, I could not gather...

...Their impression at first had been that they were destined to be devoured by the white men, and they were reluctant to eat, fearing it was intended to fatten them for that doom."

—Pascoe G. Hill: *Fifty Days on Board a Slave-Vessel*

"The sales in North America tended to differ from those in the islands. Slaves were sold on board ship, the sales spread over sevral days. Those sold departed with their new owners; the others returned to their chains to await the next sale. Slaves in Virginia often endured numerous sales, each with their inhuman inspection, the worries and uncertainties, and the sad departure of friends and shipmates. A slaver might take up to two and a half months to sell a complete cargo, the healthy men go first, the sick last of all. Even then, the traveling was not over. Unlike slaves on the Waccamaw rice plantations, Africans destined for the Chesapeake tobacco plantations often had to walk [barefooted] for miles in the wake of the new owner or agent.

In South Carolina and Virginia... slaves were shipped onwards, along the extensive river networks and waterways, to their immediate destinations, thence inland to another colony."

—James Walvin: *Black Ivory*

The Africans from the New Land rowed the small boat smoothly, quietly and consciously looked away from your naked body. There were about forty of you who were separated on board the Slaveship and brought over to this New Land which you are now beginning to smell, a rancid torture-smell.

You are the only woman. What fate lies ahead? What violent and sexual fantasies does the grinning lustful white man want from you? No one speaks your language. You are frustrated. Angry. Alone in your determination to be Free... or so you think.

But what does FREEDOM mean now in this whiteman's land? Can you ever return Home alive? If you did, could you slip pass the Hunters and return to your *Seke* village? And what would you find? You remember with vivid clarity the fires and chaos of screams, blood, gunshots, whips...

As you are dreamingly drifting on about Home and being led off onto the New Land's shore, one of the New Land Africans hands you a cloth to cover your nakedness, steadies your still sea-wobbling body and whispers to you in your native toungue:

"Peace and Strength, my Sister!"

You are speechless. It has been months since you've spoken to another Seke.

"I am Oludin. But the whiteman calls me 'Matt'. You are in a place they call 'South Carolina.' Your master will be Master Henderson some two days' boat ride up the river...."

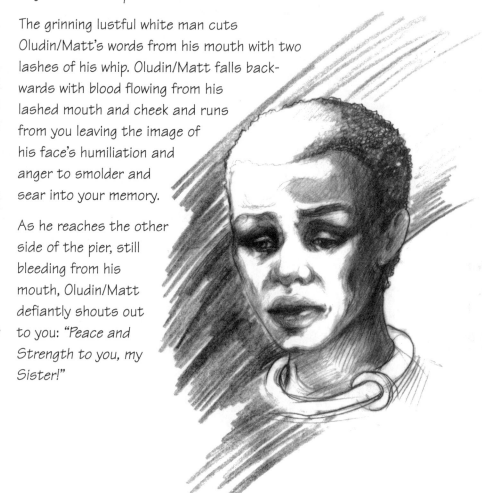

The grinning lustful white man cuts Oludin/Matt's words from his mouth with two lashes of his whip. Oludin/Matt falls backwards with blood flowing from his lashed mouth and cheek and runs from you leaving the image of his face's humiliation and anger to smolder and sear into your memory.

As he reaches the other side of the pier, still bleeding from his mouth, Oludin/Matt defiantly shouts out to you: "Peace and Strength to you, my Sister!"

A NEW AFRICAN:

"SEASONED" AND TALKING LIKE A WHITE MAN

For a moment you are not alone: A Seke man survives in this New Land! Then you are twisted around by a fierce looking African man in white man's clothes. He holds you with one arm and with the other he, with great authority, pokes his chest, grins and shouts as if you are deaf: "Charles!"

Soon you get to understand that he is the white man's overseer and that he will be taking you and the forty other Africans to the Henderson plantation.

Charles drags you to a shack where there are pigs and horses and other African Captives waiting their time to either be sold or taken away by the agents of their new masters. There are what looks like 30 women shoved into a corner of the shack next to the horses, but with much less space than the horses have. You could only stand shoulder to shoulder or back to back. Some women were dressed in rags, some were dressed in better clothes and a few were stark naked.

Charles shoves you into the crowd of African women of many shades of Black. A crude iron chain gate swung down from the shacks rafters almost crushing you and another Sister. You could smell putrid sickness and taste Death. It was hot and the hay scratched your legs while flies and mosquitoes swarmed you and the others...

The men had it worse. There were many more of them: about 100 or more as you could see. They were forced to sit or squat in two stalls bordered by pig stalls which seemed to have never been cleaned. That side of the shack had no windows and was furthest from the door. Worse still, there were some men who had been in the stalls for four and five days. Having no toilets, they had to relieve themselves right there. There were some very sick men sitting and leaning or trying to lie down with a few inconsiderate brothers stepping on them or trying to shove them into the corner where the makeshift toilet was.

For you, this was just another night on board the Slaveship. Just new faces with the same miseries: coughing, moaning, screaming, cursing in numerous languages, pushing, scratching, praying and calling the Spirits.

At dawn the following morning, after you realized that you survived another miserable night with two-three hours sleep, you find yourself on the river barge slowly pulling away from the pier packed with your forty shipmates, Charlie, the grinning nasty whiteman and loads of provisions.

You desperately scan the docks, buildings and streets for Oludin/Matt. Nothing.

Only a beautiful black bird with bright red and yellow tipped wings circling your barge. It sees you looking at it and dips its wing and swoops so close to your face that you can feel the breeze of its flapping wings.

Among the Seke People, certain birds are guides and reminders.

You think: *This is Oludin/Matt.*

This *Oludin-bird* is guiding you on the path of Survival and is reminding you that wherever you go, plant the Resistance Seed... and that your children and children's children will **Always Remember**...

...THE FREEDOM FIGHT IS FAR FROM OVER!

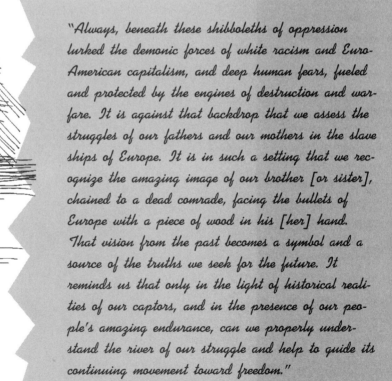

"Always, beneath these shibboleths of oppression lurked the demonic forces of white racism and Euro-American capitalism, and deep human fears, fueled and protected by the engines of destruction and warfare. It is against that backdrop that we assess the struggles of our fathers and our mothers in the slave ships of Europe. It is in such a setting that we recognize the amazing image of our brother [or sister], chained to a dead comrade, facing the bullets of Europe with a piece of wood in his [her] hand. That vision from the past becomes a symbol and a source of the truths we seek for the future. It reminds us that only in the light of historical realities of our captors, and in the presence of our people's amazing endurance, can we properly understand the river of our struggle and help to guide its continuing movement toward freedom."

—**Vincent Harding:** *There Is a River*

Within two months on the Henderson plantation; within two months of constant rapes and whippings for your "insolence" by Master Henderson and his ever-grinning son... *Oludin/Matt* finds you, loves you in those tense passionfilled night moments or stolen daysnatches in the field just beyond that crazy bend in the James River, talks to you of Freedomschemes, teaches you English and how to read from the Bible. Little Master Henderson catches you returning from one of your fiercely tender moments together and immediately sells you to a Virginia tavern owner looking for a good "breeder."

You try to hold back the tears as you sit among the tavern master's rum kegs and other provisions on the back of his noisy rickety wagon. You and *Oludin/Matt* knew there could not be lasting relations in this Hell, but you both wished those joyful touches, laughs, swiftsmiles, firey fingers, and black bodies moulding into one Lovebeing would go on forever and ever. Tears because you know a Freedomseed has been planted in you, heart & soul nourishing your mind... and the African warrior growing within you....

You name your firstborn son *Oludin/Gabriel* because you know he will be a powerful man. He is born in that powerful year of 1776; when whites talked of, fought for, and snagged their freedom from British rule. Now they are free to keep you enslaved without paying tribute to their Motherland. When *Oludin/Gabriel* was only a week old, you convinced Master Prosser that you would be a better profit maker for him if you could tend to the tavern and its patrons rather than be sold out as a breeder. But he still was greedy. He forced you to "breed" two more children, *Ademu/Solomon* and *Kotuse/Martin*. You begged, pleaded, got down on your knees and successfully persuaded Master Prosser not to sell the young ones once they were weaned.

... Because you had a Freedomplan.

"...By the time they reached their twenties, these tall, sturdy young men knew they were meant to be free, and they were prepared to wage hard and decisive struggle for that costly freedom, not only for themselves but for others as well.

In the spring of 1800, as the sharp, sometimes fiercely divisive sounds of the white Federalist and Republican debates echoed through the states, the Virginia brothers and their comrades began to organize among their people, and the leadership passed finally to Gabriel's hands. At twenty-four he was the youngest— and the tallest, standing well over six feet. With his dark complexion, prominent scars, and Ethiopian features, he was a striking figure... White authorities did not know Gabriel's rank in life, but his fellow Africans did, for by the summer he and his two brothers had gathered an impressive cadre of comrades for the proposed struggle. Under the cover of funerals and other black religious gatherings, and in the hours after sundown when the exiled African community reaffirmed its integrity through singing and praying and loving and planning and escaping— in those times and hours, Gabriel presented his [and his mother's] plan. It was strategically simple and seemed sound. [On August 30, 1800] Several hundred men would make a surprise midnight attack on Richmond to capture arms, burn warehouses, and perhaps take the governor as hostage, thereby inspiring a general uprising among thousands of Africans...."

—**Vincent Harding:** *There Is a River*

You, **Adun** (Shekiri for "one who struggles alone"), of the proud *Seke* people
have sucessfully planted and nurtured
the **Freedomseed**. You, **Adun**, Survivor
of the MiddlePassage have remembered
to pass on *The Plan* whispered on that
terror-filled first day on board the
Deathship. You, **Adun**, know, whether or
not your sons succeed in their strike for
Freedom, our struggle will move forward
and deepen among the Captive Africans
throughout this vast land.

Adun, the lone struggler who was and is not alone,
knows **we are all in this "Black River of Struggle."**
We pay tribute to her, her sons, those who preced-
ed her as fighters and those who followed fighting:
we will **always remember** by continuing to plant
the **Freedomseed**.

> "Who controls the past controls the future;
> Who controls the present controls the past."
> —George Orwell, *1984*

PART 5:

IN SEARCH OF THE
REAL
NUMBERS

How many Africans were actually killed or taken from their homeland by the European Slave Trade?

It is not surprising that the West has systematically presumed the right to define, describe, rationalize, and downplay the magnitude of the African Holocaust—but what *is* surprising is that so many scholars who take pride in their independent thinking have been duped by it. What is even more astonishing is that it never occurred to the the best of our scholars that accepting corporate white America's self-serving definition of the Black Holocaust was the equivalent of allowing the Nazis to define the Jewish Holocaust.

According to the "official" "academically approved," "definitive" study of the African slave trade by **Philip Curtain** (*The African Slave Trade: A Census*), the total number of enslaved Africans imported to the Americas from 1451–1870 [419 years], was 9,566,000. Roughly 10 million. According to Mr. Curtain, some two million Africans died (during capture, the MiddlePassage, etc.)

In recent years, descendants of the victims took it upon themselves to do their own research, to conduct their own search for truth, and to speak on their Ancestors' behalf instead of letting self-serving Western scholars speak for them. Progressive African and African-American scholars such as Joseph Inikori, the late Walter Rodney, Ivana Elb, Charles Becker, David Richardson, and Joseph Becker—along with openminded non-Blacks like British historian Basil Davidson—have, through their research, begun to confirm what Black social science pioneer activist-scholar W.E.B. Dubois estimated over a hundred years ago: the number of Africans killed and enslaved during the Atlantic Slave Trade was far larger than whitewashed numbers usually given—the number was *enormous!*

Since Curtin's original assertions, the previously mentioned scholars have gone beyond the all-too-often-whitewashed official records of the Slave Trade companies and their respective countries. The relentless new scholars have examined in great detail the log books of slaveship captains and doctors, along with diaries (which often reveal truths that official records conceal); they (Mr. Inihori in particular) have identified at least six different categories of British slave vessels, some of which were never tallied into the official numbers; they have crosschecked newspaper reports and slaveship captains' diaries against the "official" numbers. Armed with new methodology and assumptions, these scholars and others have concluded that, for example:

The French Slave Trade was underestimated by a full 50%!

The early Portuguese (1450-1521) Slave Trade was actually *double* Curtain's estimate for the same period.

The volume of the 18th century British Slave Trade was at least 1/4 to 1/3 larger than Curtain's estimate.

It is not unreasonable to assume that further research will turn up similar discrepancies as it focuses on different periods of the Slave Trade and on the different European nations involved. If we add to that (or multiply by) the assertion that for every African that lived to reach the Americas, five others died during the struggle to take them by force, during the famines and the forced marches to the coast, during their incarceration in the barracoons and slave dungeons, during the obscene brutality of the MiddlePassage and during their attempts to escape every step of the way...

After 500 years of that...

...how many deaths...?

If we look again at the rough census track from 1650 to 1900 of Africa, Europe, and Asia—and do a little simple math—we get a truly horrifying picture...

The census below gives the population in the millions:

	1650	1750	1850	1900
Africa	100	100	100	120
Europe	103	144	274	423
Asia	257	437	656	857

Clearly, if Africa had grown at the same rate as Europe and Asia, Africa would have had a population of some 400 million by 1900—but Africa's population was only 120 million.

To Professor Curtin (and all the other apologists for slavery) we ask: What happened to the other *280 million* Africans who should have been alive in Africa in 1900? To say the least, these numbers imply a tremendous loss of life of the people of Africa—one that the West has not even begun to come to terms with.

In light of the "missing" 280 million—pardon me, I failed to subtract the 10 million whose enslavement Mr.Curtain acknowledges—in the light of the *"missing" 270 million Africans*, it is obvious that the estimate of W.E.B. DuBois, Walter Rodney, Cheik Anta Diop, Joseph Inikori and other Black scholars (as well as the British Historian Basil Davidson), that between 50 and 100 million African lives were lost, was...very, VERY conservative.

THE SLAUGHTER OF OVER
100 MILLION
AFRICAN MEN, WOMEN,
CHILDREN?
THE ENSLAVEMENT OF
MILLIONS OF OTHERS?

THAT IS THE BLACK HOLOCAUST.

AfterWord...

This book has focused on the capture of Africans for the Slave Trade; their experience traveling to the dungeons on the coastlines of West and East Africa; their sufferings and resistance within those dungeons of torture, humiliation, and death; THEIR SUFFERINGS AND RESISTANCE ON THE SLAVESHIPS DURING THE HORRENDOUS MIDDLEPASSAGE; OF BEING PICKED OVER AND SOLD during the Scramble or on the auction block for the new experience of creating the first people of the Modern Era: **African Americans, Afrolatinos, AfroCaribbeans.**

We did not have the space to look at the "slavery experience in the Americas" itself. That experience requires another book: **Slavery For Beginners. The Black Holocaust For Beginners** described the experiences that brought our ancestors to the shores of the Americas.

We wanted to disturb you. Incite you. Give you insight. Inform you. We wanted you to **always remember** that millions and millions of African People lost their lives, were maimed, or went crazy during the 1400 years of the African Slave Trade that was central in the creation of the present World Economic System.

We wanted the reader to begin to sense all the terrible things... brutal, beastly things of the Capture and MiddlePassage. We also wanted the reader to experience the defiance and resistance that was the dominant feeling among the Captive Africans. **We were chained, shackled and yoked not because of our passivity, but because of our resistance... our constant struggle to be free!**

We wanted you to also see the complexity of the Black Holocaust and the development of modern slavery as an essential component in the development of the present World Economic System. Today, on those rare occasions when we do hear or read about the Black Holocaust and Slavery, the reality is often simplified, trivialized and distorted to present these gross experiences as aberations or quirks in the fundamentally moral development of Western Civilization and its attempts to "bring civilization to the African savages." Even Donald Duck's Disney Productions wants to capitalize on our genocidal enslavement by depicting the "fun and games" of slavery within an "American History" Theme Park! After reading this book, you know better. You know the **Black Holocaust** was neither trivial nor incidental.

Ultimately, we hope *The Black Holocaust For Beginners* will help you look at this period in our History of Resistance and Struggle, to dig deeper so as to learn and be inspired to join in the legacy of being Freedomfighters, Liberators, Keepers of the Moral High Ground....

SLAVE DUNGEON
UP TO 1790's

PART 6:

What You Can Do To Continue Our Legacy of Resistance & Struggle... Our *"Movement Toward Freedom"*

"We are Africans not because we are born in Africa, but because Africa is born in us. Look around you and behold us in our Greatness. Greatness is an African Possibility; you can make it yours."
—Chester Higgins, Jr.: **Feeling the Spirit**. Bantam Books. 1994

Reading this book and relating to its powerful images is not enough. Telling your children, relatives and friends about this book is not enough.

You must *act*.

Join in on the various cultural and political efforts to Remember and Demand Reparations long overdue. Some of the activities and organizations are listed below, but the list does not cover all that is avaliable. So be on the lookout for activities in your neighborhood and spread the word.

PARTICIPATE IN A MIDDLEPASSAGE COMMEMORATION® CEREMONY

The MiddlePassage Commemoration® is a ceremony developed by Sisters Sandra Gould Ford, Dr. Huberta Jackson-Lowman and Bisi Hightower of Pittsburgh, Pa. to help us *Always Remember.* They suggest that we can perform this ceremony throughout the year. However, it is traditionally observed during the so-called "Thanksgiving" weekend. It is our hope that this ceremony will gain in popularity just as *Kwanzaa* has.

GOALS

To acknowledge and document the social and psychological impact of the MiddlePassage—

To help us join in the struggle to create a better future based on our timeless Creativity before this history of terror, genocide and resistance—

To further develop and promote ceremonies, traditions and events that build awareness and appreciation for the Black Experience of Survival and Creativity, Resistance and Struggle—

ITEMS NEEDED–

Earthen bowl or pan with salt water to represent the Atlantic Ocean.

Small boat or floating vessel to be placed in the bowl or pan to represent the legacy of African navigational skill and the Slaveship.

Silver items and imitation jewelery to represent the sale of our Ancestors into slavery.

Chains baked from rolled cookie dough. These symbolize the chains that bound us into slavery and remind us that our African Ancestors did not go into slavery passively (pretzels could be substitued for cookie dough).

Rocks, grass and dirt for our spiritual respositories and to represent our Ancestral homeland: Mother Africa.

Wooden Matches to convey our political and cultural awareness and our boundless vitality.

Display these items in a specially prepared space in your house

EACH PARTICIPANT SHOULD BRING–

Materials for creating artwork: paper, fabric, paints and/or ink, trinkets, seeds, beans, buttons, glue....

A white candle respresenting the bones of the millions of Africans who perished during the MiddlePassage.

A covered dish representing food enjoyed by a forbearer. A sampling of each item is placed on a special platter in honor of the Ancestors.

THE CEREMONY

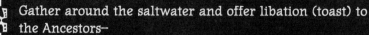

Gather around the saltwater and offer libation (toast) to the Ancestors–

Light all candles, then offer prayers and/or praises for the Ancestors and our forebears, seeking their guidance–

"Sail" a "vessel" across the water to remember the free exploration and trade throughout the Americas by Africans whose navigational charts made Columbus' trip possible–

"Sail" again to memorialize the centuries of African enslavement and the genocidal horrors of the MiddlePassage. Blow out all but one candle that repre- sents our physical, cultural and spiritual losses. Use the single lit candle to relight all of the other candles to rep- resent the rekindling of our struggle to be free from gen- eration to generation.

Say prayers and/or praises to guide and protect the young and unborn who follow us.

The Chains are broken and consumed and there is the making of joyful noise, such as songs, drumming, dances or other expressions of joy–

There is a final group activity that begins, completes or displays a creative project.

NOTE. *Some suggestions to help us to always remember the horrors and struggles of our Ancestors during the MiddlePassage: The family or families could begin or complete a MiddlePassage quilt, exhibit other artwork from each of the participants. The matches used could be painted or inked by the children–supervised by an adult– with our Liberation colors: Red, Black, Green, Yellow or Gold.*

For more information on the **MiddlePassage Commemoration**® contact:
Sister Sandra Gould Ford
Shooting Star Productions
7123 Race St.
Pittsburgh, PA 15208–1424
412. 731. 7464

GROUPS TO WORK WITH CONCERNING...
THE BLACK HOLOCAUST, BLACK GENOCIDE AND
REPARATIONS:

African Holocaust Newsletter
Omar Ali-Bey– Founder
6122 Woodlland Avenue
Cleveland, Oh 44104
216. 881. 9741 or 881. 5433

*America's Black Holocaust
Museum*
James Cameron– Founder/Director
2233 N. 4th Street
Milwaukee, WI 53212
414. 264. 2500

Black Reparations Commission
Box 1397
Rockville, MD 20849-1397
301. 279. 9235

*National Coalition of Black For
Reparations (N'COBRA)*
Box 75437
Baton Rouge, LA 70874
504. 355. 1156

AFRAM newsservices
Preston Wilcox– Editor/Curator
2322 Third Ave.
Harlem, NY 10035
212. 281. 3055

*The African Burial Ground
Committee*
Office of Public Education and
Interpretation of the African Burial
Ground
6 World Trade Center, Room 239
New York, NY 10048

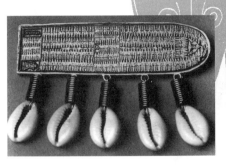

*If you desire a gold, silver or brass
pin depicting the Slaveship "Brookes"
as shown on the back of this book
and on the title page, contact:*

Who Deserves It More Than You?
Sista Phyllis M. Bowdwin
Box 1361
Bronx, NY 10451
718. 367. 5233

We need to visit the **Great Blacks In
Wax** Museum
*1601-03 E. North Ave.
Baltimore, Md. 21213*

The museum not only has striking
lifelike wax replicas of famous
African-American historical figures,
it also has a powerfully moving
exhibit of a typical slaveship that
leaves no one untouched. You should
make an effort to bring your family
and friends to *our* wax museum. It
cannot survive without your visits!

READING LIST

(• = highly recommended reading)

MOLEFI K. ASANTE & MARK T. MATTSON **Historical and Cultural Atlas of African Americans**. Macmillan, New York. 1992.

RONALD BAILEY *"The Slave(ry) Trade and the Development of Capitalism in the United States: the Textile Industry in New England"* in *Social Science History*, Vol. 14, Issue 3, Fall 1990.

DR HILARY BECKLES & VERENE SHEPHERD **Caribbean Slave Society and Economy**. The New Press, New York. 1993.

LERONE BENNETT, JR. **Before the Mayflower**. Penguin Books, New York. 1993.

J. CAUGHTRY **The Notorious Triangle**. Temple University Press, Philadelphia. 1981.

John Henrik Clarke **Christopher Columbus & the Afrikan Holocaust**. A & B Books, Brooklyn, NY. 1992.

STANLEY F. CHYET **Lopez of Newport**. Wayne State University Press, Detroit. 1970.

BASIL DAVIDSON **The African Slave Trade**. Little, Brown, Boston. 1980.

• **The Search for Africa**. Times Books, New York. 1994.

Transatlantic Slavery Against Human Dignity. National Museum & Galleries of Merryside, Liverpool, England. 1994.

• CHEIKH ANTA DIOP **Civilization or Barbarism**. Lawrence Hill Books, New York. 1991.

• John Hope Franklin **From Slavery to Freedom**. Alfred A. Knopf, New York. 1967.

David Barry Gaspar **Bondmen and Rebels**. Duke University Press, Durham. 1992.

Elizabeth Gordan **Slavery and the Slave Trade in Zanzibar**. A & B Bookstore, Brooklyn, NY.

• Murray Gordon **Slavery In The Arab World**. New Amsterdam. New York. 1992.

Ida Hakim **Reparations: The Cure for America's Race Problem**. UB & US Communications Systems. 1994.

Vincent Harding **There Is a River– The Black Struggle for Freedom in America**.Harcourt Brace Janovich, New York. 1981.

Chester Higgins, Jr. **Feeling the Spirit**. Bantam Books. 1994.

• Pascoe G. Hill **Fifty Days On Board a Slave-Vessel**. Black Classic Press, Baltimore. 1993.

Joseph E. Inikori *"The Chaining of a Continent: Export Demand for Captives and the History of Africa South of the Sahara, 1450 – 1870."* Institute of Social and Economic Research, University of the West Indies, Mona, Kinston 7, Jamaica. 1992.

– **Forced Migration**. Africana Publishing Company, New York. 1982.

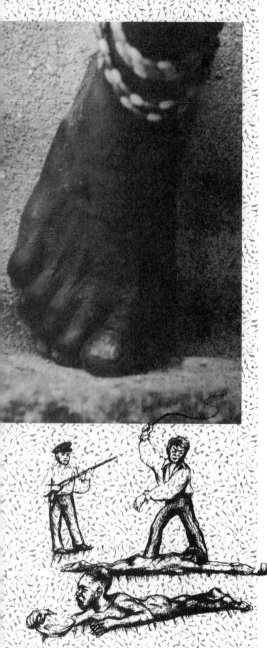

— "The Volume of the British Slave Trade, 1655 – 1807" in *Cahiers d' etudes africaines, No. 128, Vol, XXXII, Issue 4, 1992.*

• • JOSEPH E. INIKORI & STANLEY L. ENGERMAN, EDS. **The Atlantic Slave Trade**. Duke University Press, Durham. 1992.

PETER KOLCHIN **American Slavery: 1619 – 1877**. Hill and Wang, New York. 1993.

• BERNARD LEWIS **Race and Slavery in the Middle East**. Oxford University Press. 1990.

LOUISE LEVATHES **When China Ruled the Seas**. Simon & Schuster, New York. 1994.

• SIDNEY MINTZ & RICHARD PRICE **The Birth of African-American Culture**. Beacon Press, Boston. 1992.

E. JEFFERSON MURPHY **History of African Civilization**. Thomas Y. Crowell, New York. 1972.

• REPARATIONS PETITION **For United Nations Assistance Under Resolution 1503 (XLVIII) – On Behalf of African Americans In The United States of America**. 912 West Pembroke Ave. Hampton, VA 23669. UB & US Communications Systems. 1994.

WALTER RODNEY **How Europe Underdeveloped Africa**. Bogle-L'Ouverture, London. 1972. Howard University Press, Washington. 1980.

• **Kofi Baadu Out of Africa**. Working Peoples Alliance, Georgetown, Guyana. 1980.

DAVID SMITH & PHIL EVANS **Kapital For Beginners**. Writers & Readers, New York. 1982.

• BRENDA E. STEVENSON, *"Slavery,"* in **Black Women in America,** Vol. II. Eds. Darlene Clark Hine, Elsa Barkely Brown, Rosalyn Terborg-Penn. Indiana University Press. 1994.

LISBETH GANT STEVENSON **African American History: Heroes In Hardship**. Cambridgeport Press, Cambridge, MA. 1992.

• HERMAN J. VIOLA & CAROLYN MARGOLIS **Seeds of Change**. Smithsonian Institution Press, Washington. 1991.

JAMES WALVIN **Black Ivory.** Howard University Press, Washington, D.C. 1992.

• ERIC WILLIAMS **Capitalism & Slavery.** Capricorn Books, New York. 1966.

TO MALE
DUNGEON

CHAIN WAVES

I

I went to Riis Beach and Put my ear to the ocean
I went to Atlantic City and Put my ear to the ocean
I went to Chesapeake Bay and Put my ear to the ocean

I went to the South Sea Islands and Put my ear to

                                            Clapboardwalls

I heard chains inside the ocean's roar
I heard Bones whitened by salty time rattlin for blackskin
I heard different moanblues in Yoruba, Ibo, Akan, Bantu

I heard transformed memories and tears drop from ashy

                                            seaswept faces

I looked into Jamestown waters and Saw
Blackbones beckoning me in rhythm to a Jr Walker wail
I looked into Savannah waters and saw
Blackhusbands hugging sister/mothers crying-cradling their

                                            unborn

I looked into the Everglades and Bayou Swamps and Saw
rusted rifles clenched by deathfists fortelling Brother Nat

I looked thru clapboard walls and Saw
Gabriel's ghost whispering Revolt in my ears.

II

In the Sunrise East no winds blew
       but the sea was restless
In the Sunrise East no clouds passed
       but the air darkened—
       anticipating War
In the Sunrise East I looked behind me:
       the skyline America with brothers
       and sisters taking their places

In the sunrise East no shadows prevailed
just mahogany memorybones salted and searching
for ebonyflesh in Revenge and Humanity.

III

and now our bonesisters *feel*
and now our bonebrothers *feel*
it is time they rise up:
we had called for them in our ancestral wails
thru Bessie, Shine, Nina, Tbone, Curtis...

and now our fleshless fighters make
the tide rise inspite of the whitemoon

we had fought without Them and within Them
Now we fight with Them as Them... as Us
and now Black Bonetide **Rise!** crackling
       against Carib shores and Bahia—
       defying the arrogant Lunalust
       pulling against the Namibian and Azanian shores.

The flaming chain waves of our unity with all of us
cut the invisible shackles of moontide
flooding the steelglass caves and canyons of the Snowpeople
melting the Deathsoul into Sodomdeath
Roasting maggotthoughts clearing the Earth's air
for us to breathe and recreate
what Coltrane spearwhispered to us — *Spitirtual Unity*
what Shango kept chanting to Harriet, Albizu & Maceo— *Liberation*
for us to breathe and recreate
what Allah hummed to Malcolm— *SelfDetermination*
for us to breathe and recreate *Okra* and *Nommo*
                      and *Peace*

                          —S.E. Anderson

ABOUT THE AUTHOR
S. E. Anderson

Photo by Suliman Ellison

S. E. Anderson, a veteran activist/educator, has been involved in the Black Liberation Movement on many levels. He is not only a mathematics professor, a Senior Editor (*NOBO*: *Journal of African American Dialogue*), a founding member of the Network of Black Organizers and of The African Heritage Studies Association but also an essayist on a variety of topics related to Black culture and liberation as well as science and technology. His political and cultural activism in his native New York City ranges from helping to found the New York City Algebra Project to being a founding member of the *New York City Coalition For Excellence In Black Education*.

As a young activist, Anderson was a member of the Student Nonviolent Coordinating Committee (SNCC) and helped found the Black Panther Party in Harlem in 1966. He has been active in the African Liberation

Support Movement since 1964 and participated in the historic Black student/community struggle against Columbia University's encroachment into Harlem in 1968. Ironically, almost twenty years later, he became a Columbia University Revson Fellow (1986-7). In addition, he has taught mathematics, science, and Black Studies at Queens College....

Anderson became one of the first Black Studies Chairs, when in 1969 he accepted the challenge at Sarah Lawrence College to create a department that included mathematics and the natural sciences as part of a Black Studies Curriculum.

Currently, Anderson is working on two books: **Race For Beginners** and **Slavery For Beginners**. He is also collaborating with Sri Lankan scientist Susantha Goonitilake on a **World Science For Beginners** book.

S. E. Anderson lives in Harlem with his activist/writer wife–Rosemari Mealy. They have two sons–Dedan and Marc.

CRO-MAAT is a new arts collective consisting of seven aspiring artists.

Specialties: Graphic Design, Photography, Illustration
Phone (212) 473-4706

In the beginning we were several individuals soaking up knowledge as we swam the seas of information. Each from different ethnic backgrounds, we sought art as a means to express ourselves in our different cultural situations. With art as our common means of communication, we found that we could strengthen our message as a union. This is Cro-Maat.

As we make our debut in ***The Black Holocaust For Beginners***, we look ahead to producing many other works to display truth by means of imagery.

Thank you, Writers and Readers.

Shawn Alexander   Wangechi Mutu
Khalid Best   Luis Perez
Juan Gutierrez   Lorena Persade
Gregory St. Amand

INDEX

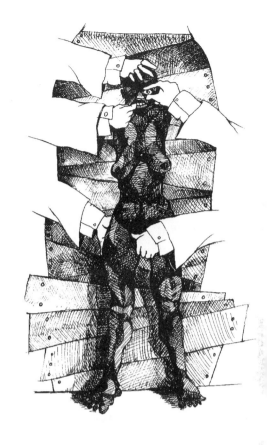

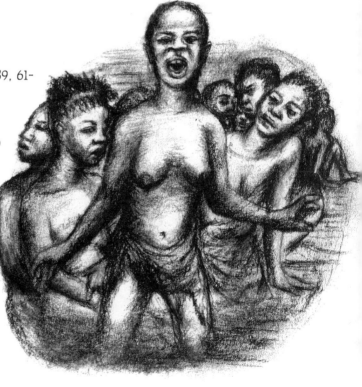

183